Dwayne's Guitar Lessons Presents:

How To Play Guitar Solos

By

Dwayne Jenkins

Copyright © 2020 Dwayne Jenkins.
All Rights Reserved.
Published by Tritone Publishing

Introduction

Have you ever wanted to play guitar solos? Have you ever listened to a song and when it gets to the lead break you get excited? Have you ever wondered if it was possible for you to be able to do that? Well you know what? It is.

The lead guitar break has always been an exciting part of the song. It is where the guitar player gets to shine. It is where he gets to sing with his guitar and make really cool sounds that make you go "I want to do that."

But where do you start with playing guitar solos? You see them wiz all over the fretboard and sound good with every note they play. How do they do it? What sacred musical knowledge do they possess to be able to do that?

Well, to be honest with you, it's not quite as hard as it seems. If you know the right concepts and techniques that relate to the art of playing guitar solos, you can do it too. You just need to know where to look and what to play.

<u>How To Play Guitar Solos</u> is that place to look and that place to start. It will show you the concepts and fundamental principles that are used by all lead guitar players to play guitar solos that sound awesome.

You will learn a simple easy way to approach playing guitar solos. You will learn how to bring them to life and play them anywhere on the fretboard you choose to do so. And in the process, you will learn how to stay in key.

One of the main issues I see students having when attempting to play guitar solos, is knowing when and where to play them. Even if they get guidance as to when, they still need to know where. And this is where they falter. You must know where to play your guitar solo in order to sound correct.

Even if you learn a scale or two, you have to play them in the right spot at the right time. If not, the notes you play will sound terrible. Your listener will be putting their hands to their ears and looking at you as if to say "take some lessons".

Of course you don't want that. What you want them to say is "wow, that sounds awesome!" This training guide will help you to accomplish that. Of course you need to study and practice. But if you do, look out world because here you come.

Dwayne Jenkins

Table of contents

Introduction

Chapter 1 Getting Started   1

Lesson 1: The guitar scale   1
Lesson 2: Lead guitar specialty   3
Lesson 3: Important scales to know   4
Lesson 4: Reading tabs   7
Lesson 5: Finger exercises   11
Chapter 1 Summary   14

Chapter 2 Major Pentatonic Scales   15

Lesson 6: Major pentatonic scale #1   15
Lesson 7: Major pentatonic scale #2   17
Lesson 8: Major pentatonic scale #3   19
Lesson 9: Major pentatonic scale #4   21
Lesson 10: Major pentatonic scale #5   22
Chapter 2   Summary   23

Chapter 3 Minor Pentatonic Scales   25

Lesson 11: Minor pentatonic scale #1   25
Lesson 12: Minor pentatonic scale #2   27
Lesson 13: Minor pentatonic scale #3   29
Lesson 14: Minor pentatonic scale #4   31
Lesson 15: Minor pentatonic scale #5   33
Chapter 3   Summary   35

Chapter 4 Guitar Solo Techniques   37

Lesson 16: Hammer-ons   37
Lesson 17: Pull-offs   39
Lesson 18: Bends & slides   41
Lesson 19: Vibrato & trills   44
Chapter 4   Summary   46

Chapter 5: When To Play The Scales   49

Lesson 20: Song intro   49
Lesson 21: Song middle section   51
Lesson 22: Song outro   53
Lesson 23: Acapella   55
Lesson 24: Harmonizing   57
Chapter 5   Summary   60

Chapter 6 Where To Play The Scales   63

Lesson 25: Key of G major/minor   63
Lesson 26: Key of A major/minor   72
Lesson 27: Key of B major/minor   74
Lesson 28: Key of D major/minor   77
Lesson 29: Key of E major/minor   79
Chapter 6   Summary   81

Chapter 7 Learning From Recordings   83

Lesson 30: Ear training   83
Lesson 31: Practice habits   87
Lesson 32: Looping the song   91
Lesson 33: Listening for effects   92
Lesson 34: Common guitar pedals   93
Chapter 7   Summary   96

Chapter 8: Improvising   99

Lesson 35: Guitar Licks   99
Lesson 36: Transposing   103
Lesson 37: Playing arpeggios   104
Lesson 38: Alternate and tremolo picking   107
Lesson 39: Chord progressions to solo over   109
Chapter 8   Summary   115

Guitar Scales For Beginners Quiz: 119

Guitar Scales For Beginners Conclusion: 125

Chapter 1 Getting Started

Lesson 1: The guitar scale

When it comes to playing guitar solos, you want to learn scales. Very much like when you play rhythm guitar, you want to learn chords. The guitar scale is what allows you to create solos and melody lines in the music.

The guitar consists of thousands of scales. Can you believe that? I know, crazy huh? But it's true. Although there are thousands that can be learned, we don't need to learn them all. We just need to learn a few of the most common.

And the ones that are the most common to start with are the pentatonic scales. Why? Well, because there are only 5 of them and they are used by all the great guitar players. They can also be used in multiple styles of music.

In fact, they are probably being used by some of your favorite rock guitar players. People like Jimi Hendrix, Jimmy Page, Slash, Angus Young, etc, etc,etc. Almost all rock guitar solos from multiple eras use these scales. So it is a great place to start learning from.

The guitar scale is a selection of notes taken out of musical keys. Like say for instance, the key of G major. Or the Key of A minor. The musical alphabet that all western music is derived from uses 12 notes and it is these 12 notes that all music is created.

Now, to keep things simple and easy to learn we're not going to get into a lot of technical jargon. There are plenty of books out there that can do that. Here we are going to keep things simple so that we can learn quickly and easily.

For this introduction to learning to play guitar solos, we'll just figure the scale is the selection of notes that we want to learn and which ones need to be taken out of a certain key that we choose to play in.

This is why I chose to teach you the pentatonic scales. These scales do all this work for us. These particular selections of notes in any key form in such a way on the fretboard, that the notes automatically line up. This takes out the guesswork.

Pretty cool huh?

Lesson 2: Lead guitar specialty

The specialty of the lead guitarist is to provide the melody that accompanies the rhythm. Either one guitar player will create the rhythm and another create a melody or melodies to go with it. Or, both positions will be filled by one guitar player.

It can be done either way. But regardless of how it is done, the lead guitarist's specialty is to have a complete understanding of the concept of melody. The notes that will fit the rhythm.

Each rhythm progression is usually written within a specific key and it is the job of the lead guitar player to pick notes within this key that will work in harmony with that rhythm and create a melody that is pleasant to the ear.

This can only be done by knowing what to play, when to play, and where to play it no matter where you are located along the fretboard. This will be your specialty. Your contribution to the musical concept.

As a lead guitar specialist, you'll be able to identify what scale will work best in any particular situation. In any key that you choose to solo in and how to bring those scale notes to life. With such techniques as hammer-ons, pull-offs, bends, etc.

Lesson 3: Important scales to know

When it comes to guitar scales and playing lead guitar, you want to start with the foundation. The chromatic scale. This scale makes up all the notes in western music. These 12 notes will be the root of the tree so to speak.

The 12 notes of the musical alphabet or chromatic scale are: A A# B C C# D D# E F F# G G#. All scales will be created out of these 12 notes. So you want to make sure that you learn and retain this information. Look at them like twelve roots of the music tree.

Out of these twelve notes, we will choose 8 notes to create the tree trunk. This will be the Do Re Mi Fa So La Te Do that we are so familiar with from childhood. And if not, don't worry I'll show you. This is what's called the major scale.

Now out of the 8 notes of the major scale, we get what I like to call, tree branches. The 5 notes of the pentatonic scale. This goes with any key. It is these 5 notes that we will be working with in this book. They are easy to learn and work with multiple styles of music.

As I said, the major scale (tree trunk) is constructed of 8 notes. So for example the C major scale would be constructed of the C D E F G A B & C. This creates the Do Re Mi Fa So La Ti Do. This goes for any major scale in the musical alphabet.

Of course with different major scales the notes will change, but it will always be 8 notes and have that sound. In fact, if it doesn't have that sound, it is not a major scale. This is something you want to always remember.

Now, like I said before, you want to take 5 notes out of this scale to create the pentatonic scale. The pentatonic scale can be both major and minor. And since rock music is mostly in minor keys, the minor pentatonic scale is the most popular.

To make a major scale a minor scale, we need to flatten the third, sixth, and seventh note of that scale. So for example, if we take the A major scale A B C# D E F# G# A and we flatten the 3rd, 6th, and 7th notes, we now have A B C D E F G A.

We then take 5 notes out of this A minor scale to make the minor pentatonic scale. These notes would be the A C D E & G. These are the notes we would use to create our guitar solo in this key. You'd be surprised what can be done with 5 notes.

Of course you can use more than five notes to create a guitar solo but when it comes to the pentatonic scales, there are only 5 notes. That is what makes them so cool to start out with. Very much like your 5 basic guitar chords.

The major pentatonic scale is made up of the 1, 2, 3, 5, & 6th note of the 8 notes in the major scale it comes out of, and the minor pentatonic scale is created from the 1 b3, 4, 5, and b7 of the scale that it is derived from.

Start out with the basics and build from there. That is what this book is about. Forming a full understanding of the basic fundamentals of playing guitar solos and how to use certain notes to do so anywhere you choose to play.

This will allow you to build a solid foundation that you can continue to build on for years to come. Because there are literally thousands of scales you can learn on the guitar.

Being that's the case, let's keep it simple and start with a scale of just 5 notes. As you progress in this book, you will become aware of just how popular this scale is. So don't overlook its simplicity.

Lesson 4: Reading tabs

Tabs are a simplified style of sheet music designed for guitar. I recommend learning to read this as it will help you to visualize the scale shapes. This will also help you out with other things as well as reading chord charts and guitar riffs.

For our purposes here, we will use it to recognize the scale patterns. I say patterns because the pentatonic scale notes create patterns along the guitar fretboard and it is these patterns that make them easy to learn.

Reading tabs is very easy and once you see what I'm talking about when it comes to patterns, you'll be able to learn the scales quicker and more easily. This will allow you to get to playing faster and having more fun.

Tab consists of six horizontal lines that represent the six guitar strings. These will be from high to low. Meaning your biggest string will be the bottom line and your smallest string will be on the top. Like looking at your guitar upside down.

8

As you can see, we have six lines and they will represent the guitar strings with your sixth string (your biggest) being on the bottom of the sheet music. The reason for this is because the lowest note is always on the bottom of the sheet music.

I know, it would be easier to understand if the strings were reversed like your guitar, but I didn't design it, I just teach how to read it. Be sure to remember this because it is very important with sheet music of any kind.

Once you have this concept down, you want to think about numbers. Why? Because numbers are what will represent the frets that you place your fingers on when playing the scales and techniques needed to bring them to life.

In this example we have a note on the 3rd fret of the first string.

Here we have a note on the 8th fret of the fourth string.

This doesn't tell us the name of the note, only its location. Which will be fine for our purposes here. Later, we will look into that. But for now we want to just get the concept down of how to understand what we are looking at.

In this example we have two notes on a string that will be played one right after the other. Not together. We have a note on the 5th fret of the sixth string and we then play a note on the 8th fret of the sixth string.

Scale patterns can also be written in diagram format. Dots represent where you place your fingers instead of numbers. These two formats are what we will be working with in this training guide for easy learning.

Many guitar players play by ear, and that's ok. There are a lot of benefits to playing this way. I will discuss this later, but I believe it is also a good idea to read the written word. It will give you insights that you can't get otherwise.

By reading guitar tabs and scale pattern diagrams you will be able to recognize note location quicker and be able to find your place in the musical spectrum faster. These are two huge abilities that will benefit you tremendously.

Lesson 5: Finger exercises

Before we get into learning the guitar scales, I want to go over a very important part of learning to play the guitar. Finger exercises. These are what will allow you to get your hands and fingers in shape for playing guitar solos.

These not only help with guitar solos, but they can also benefit you in playing guitar chords as well. So it is recommended that you take some time to look this chapter over and put it to good use. As it will really help your development.

Finger exercise #1

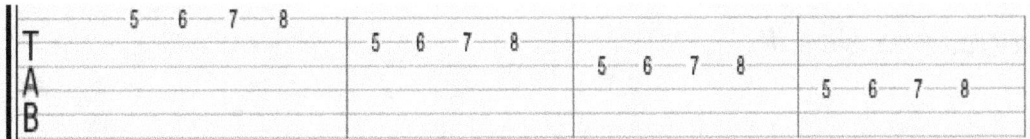

In this exercise, you use all four fingers (I strongly recommend you get the pinky in shape as well) and start on the 5th fret of the first string.

You proceed forward using all four fingers. One on each fret. Index on the 5th, middle on the 6th, ring finger on the 7th and pinky on the 8th. Go through all six strings on these four frets.

Finger exercise #2

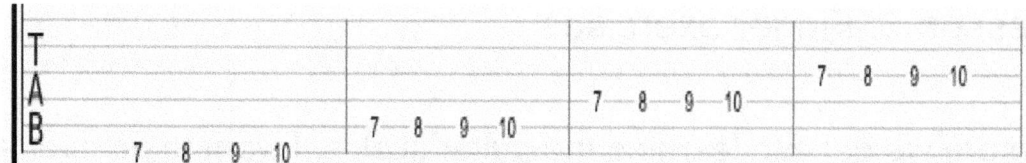

This is very similar except in reverse. You start on the sixth string and proceed down across the fretboard. Your index on the 7th fret, middle on the 8th, ring finger on the 9th, and pinky on the 10th.

Make sure to pick the notes clearly and I recommend you play these on a clean channel on the amp so you get to hear exactly what the note sounds like. Also play slowly as speed will come. Just focus on tone for right now.

Finger exercise #3

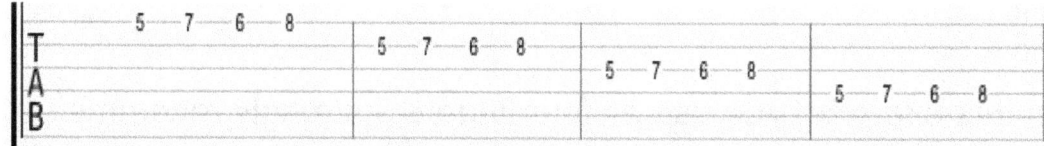

This exercise is similar to the first one except you use your fingers in a different order. Instead of 5 6 7 8, you'll do 5 7 6 8.

Finger exercise #4

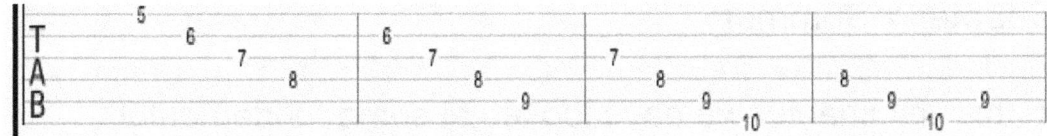

Here we do something a little different. Instead of playing four notes all on the same string, we play across four strings. We also move up the fretboard for enhanced development.

Finger exercise #5

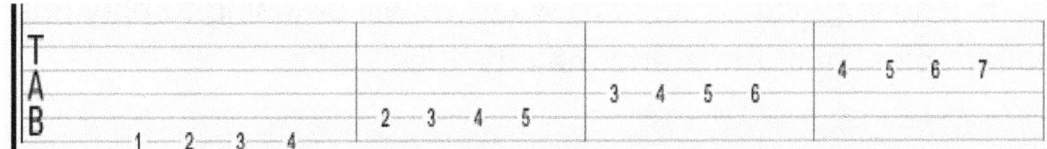

Once you have your fingers developed a bit from the first four exercises, try this one from the first fret of the sixth string. This will help build strength as the first fret is harder to push down.

These are just a few examples of what finger exercises are and how to execute them. If you work on them long enough (and I strongly suggest you do) you'll discover other options you can do as well to help your hands and fingers.

Finger exercises will develop finger independence, strength, agility, stamina, and fretboard knowledge all at the same time if you take them seriously. These will become a huge benefit to your guitar playing in all areas. So work with them daily.

Chapter 1 Summary

In this first chapter we have looked at some fundamental concepts that deal with playing guitar solos. This is most important to learn, so make sure you don't skip over this. It will only hinder your learning later on.

We first want to get a full understanding of what a guitar scale is. Because guitar scales are what we will be using to play our guitar solos, guitar riffs and melody lines.

Secondly, we want to understand the role of the lead guitar player. Just like the rhythm guitar player (sometimes both) we have a certain role we have to fulfill in the music ensemble. We must have a full understanding of this position.

In order to do this, we must have at least a basic understanding of common guitar scales that are used for this purpose. Scales such as the chromatic scale (root of all western music), the major scale, and the pentatonic scale.

And to conclude the first section of this training, we want to be able to read basic sheet music for quicker learning and practice finger exercises to get our hands and fingers in shape. These will allow us to create a solid foundation to build upon.

Chapter 2 Major Pentatonic Scales

Lesson 6: Major pentatonic scale #1

Pentatonic scales can be played in both major and minor. There are five scales and where you play these scales upon the fretboard determines whether you'll sound good or not. So we will start with the major pentatonic scales.

Below is an example of the major pentatonic scale in tab format. This scale can be played over any major chord progression in any key. You just need to know where that key is located on the fretboard.

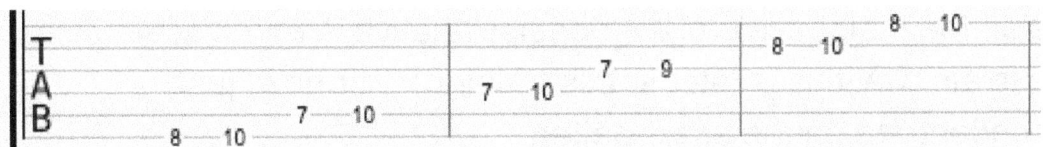

This is the major pentatonic scale pattern in the key of C major. Located at the 8th fret.

This can also be read in diagram format. I present both because people seem to lean toward one or the other. I recommend you learn both as they will help you with future learning of musical concepts.

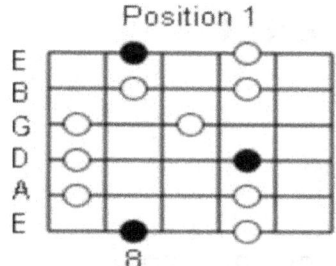

Here we have the C major pentatonic scale written in diagram format. As you can see, this is played at the 8th fret and shows you where the root notes are in this scale.

Study this box pattern. And make sure you know it back and forth. Later in the training I will show you what you can do with it to create solos.

The C major scale is the foundation for all other scales. It is also the major scale of it's popular relative A minor scale. I'll explain why this is later in this training. For now, just concentrate on the scale pattern.

Lesson 7: Major pentatonic scale #2

The second scale we want to learn is major pentatonic scale #2. What is great about these scales, is that they all present a different character, because of the way the notes are lined up on the fretboard.

Since we learned pattern #1 in the key of C major, we'll just stick with that key for this training. But once you learn all the scales, you can play them in any key and they will work like magic!

The great thing about these scales is that they connect like puzzle pieces. So if pattern #1 in the key of C major ends on the 10th fret, that means that scale pattern #2 will start exactly on the same fret that pattern #1 ended on.

Here is the second major pentatonic scale pattern. As you can see, it starts where the last one left off. On the 10th fret of the sixth string.

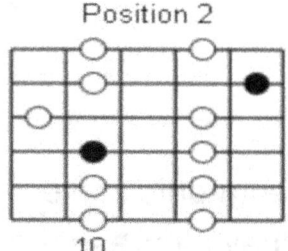

Here is the same scale pattern in diagram format. Once again, the dark dots represent where the root note (the C) is in the scale.

As you can see, it is in a different location and in only two places within the scale. This is important to know because it will give you a place to start and stop when playing guitar licks. These are how you bring the scales to life.

Remember, this pentatonic scale pattern can be played anywhere on the fretboard. It just depends on where you play it that will make the difference on whether you sound in key or not.

This is what this training will teach you. Learn that, and you will sound good every time. Why? Because you will be playing notes that come out of the key that you are playing in. And these scales make that easy because of their design.

Lesson 8: Major scale pattern #3

As you progress forward with these scale patterns, notice how they work real well together and that each one has its own character. This is because of the way the notes line up on the fretboard.

I will mention this many times because it is vitally important for you to understand this. It will give you an opportunity to express yourself in multiple ways. Although there are only five scales, what you can do with them is endless.

```
T|---------------------------------------------12--15--|
A|-------------------------------13--15----------------|
 |-------------------12--14----------------------------|
 |------------12--14-----------------------------------|
B|------12-15------------------------------------------|
 |--12-15----------------------------------------------|
```

Here is the third major pentatonic scale in the key of C major. Once again, notice how it starts where pattern 2 leaves off. At the 12th fret on the sixth string.

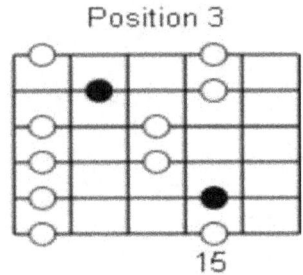

Position 3

15

Here it is written in diagram format. Once again, notice the location of the root notes. The C notes.

As I mentioned before, we will look into how we can bring these scales to life with certain techniques. But for now, just learn the scale pattern and its location within the key of C major.

Once you learn these in this key, you can then learn to transpose them into any major key you choose. No matter if it is G major, E major, A major, etc. It doesn't make a difference. And the location of the notes will take out the guesswork.

The reason why is because of their placement within the scale. As the location of the scale changes, the notes will change accordingly and allow you to sound good with ease.

Lesson 9: Major pentatonic scale #4

This next scale pattern is neat because the way the notes line up, you can naturally play an arpeggio. Now if you're not too sure what that is, don't worry I'll explain it later. For now, let's look at the 4th major pentatonic scale in C major.

```
T|----------------------------------------15--17--|
A|-----------------------------15--17-------------|
 |----------------------14--17--------------------|
B|------------14--17------------------------------|
 |----15--17--------------------------------------|
 |15--17------------------------------------------|
```

Here is the 4th major pentatonic scale starting at the 15th fret. Like all the others. It starts where #3 leaves off.

This scale can also be played at the 3rd fret for easier learning. All the scales can be played in different places, but I present this one in both positions.

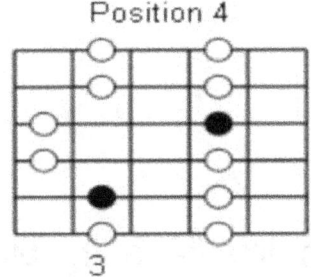

Position 4

Here is the same scale but at the 3rd fret instead of the 15th. This works because they are the same notes. The 12th fret represents the end of the scale. So all notes after that, repeat. That is why the 12th fret has two dots on it.

Lesson 10: Major pentatonic scale #5

We now come to the last of the 5 major pentatonic scales. This one is the most common out of all of them. That is because it is the first minor pentatonic scale. We will learn these in the next few lessons.

Once again, the 5th pattern is presented in two positions for easier learning. Here in tab at the 17th fret higher up on the fretboard.

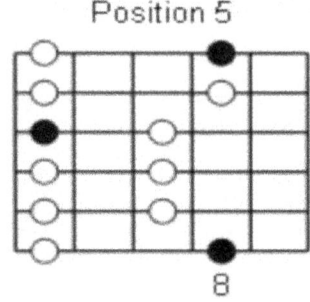

And here it is presented in the lower position (like #4) at the 5th fret with the C note on the 8th fret.

Learn these five scale patterns until you know them like the back of your hand. For they will serve you well in playing guitar solos.

Chapter 2 Summary

In this chapter we have looked at all five pentatonic scale patterns in the key of C major. I chose this scale for a particular reason. Because it has no accidentals (sharps or flats) and it is the relative major scale to A minor.

By learning the major pentatonic scale patterns in the key of C major, it will be really easy to learn the minor pentatonic scales in A minor when we get there in the next few lessons.

C major pentatonic scale pattern #1 is played at the 8th fret on the sixth string because that is where the C note is located on that string. This is very important to know for any key you choose to play in.

Pentatonic scale pattern #2 is located at the 10th fret because that is the next note in the pentatonic scale and starts where #1 leaves off.

Scale pattern #3 starts where #2 left off at. Do you remember? It is on the 12th fret. I can not stress enough the importance of you remembering this.

Number 4 is located at the 3rd and 15th frets, and scale pattern # 5 is located at the 5th and 17th frets.

24

Chapter 3 Minor Pentatonic Scales

Lesson 11: Minor pentatonic scale #1

You know what's funny? The minor pentatonic scales are the same ones. Except that they are located in a different position. Can you believe that? Crazy huh? That ought to make them easy to learn don't you think?

The most common minor scale to play these pentatonic scales in is A minor. Why? Because it is relative to the C major. Why? Because the notes are the same on each scale. That is what makes them relative. Pretty cool huh?

```
T|-----------------------------------|----------------|--------5--8--|
A|-----------------------------------|--------5--7----|--5--8--------|
A|--------------------------5--7-----|--5--7----------|--------------|
B|--5--8--------5--7-----------------|----------------|--------------|
```

This is minor pentatonic scale #1 in A minor. If you notice, it is the same pattern as #5 of the major.

*This is the most common guitar scale and used by all lead guitar players at one point or other. So make sure you learn it and learn it well.

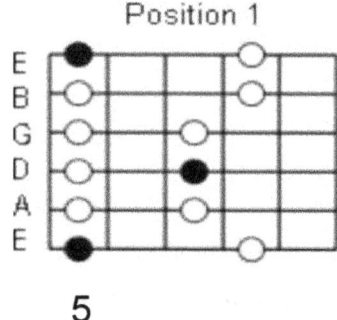

Here it is in diagram format. Notice that the root note has changed position from the major pentatonic in C. Since we're now in A minor, the root note A will be presented.

I chose to teach the major pentatonic scales first to keep things simple. C major is the easiest scale to learn and that is why I started there. A minor is the relative so that is why we continue with that scale.

Remember, they are considered relative because the two scales are made up of the same notes. This goes for all major scales.

**All major scales have a relative minor. This information will help you with creating chord progressions as well as with guitar solos.

Lesson 12: Minor pentatonic scale #2

Just like the majors, the second minor pentatonic scale starts where #1 leaves off. In the key of A minor that would be at the 8th fret. Once again, the second minor pentatonic scale is the same as the first major pentatonic scale.

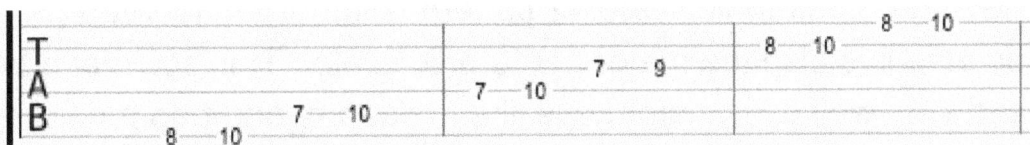

Here is pentatonic scale #2 in A minor at the 8th fet. So when you think about it, this pentatonic scale could be #1 major, or #2 minor.

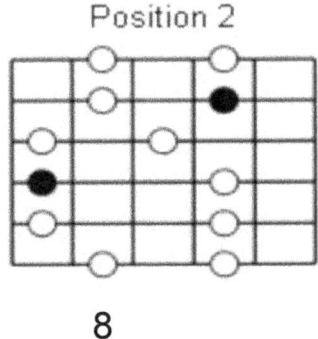

As you can see from the diagram, this starts at the 8th fret where the first minor pentatonic scale ended. Also notice the location of the root note. It is in a different position than #1. This is very important to remember.

The first two pentatonic scale patterns are the most important out of all five because of what they represent.

The minor pentatonic scale #1 pattern is the most common that people learn who play blues and rock guitar. The reason for this is because blues and rock music is in a minor key.

The minor pentatonic scale #2 pattern is important to learn because it is also the major pentatonic scale. This scale can be used very well over major keys like in country and pop music.

What is more amazing than that about these scale patterns, is that they can be used in both major and minor keys. That is why they are so common. The reason for this is because of the notes within the scales and how they line up on the fretboard.

Lesson 13: Minor pentatonic scale #3

Minor pentatonic scale pattern #3 also starts where #2 left off at the 10th fret. I mention this over and over again because it is very important that you get this down. It will make a huge difference in you being able to find these scales when you transpose to different keys.

Here we have minor pentatonic scale #3 starting at the 10th fret. Notice that it is the same as the #2 major pentatonic scale that we learned in the key of C major.

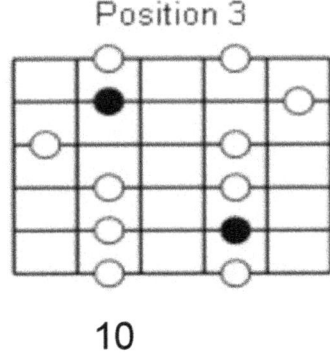

I like this pentatonic scale pattern because it has a couple of notes that step out of the box. It is these notes that give this scale its character. Also notice the placement of the root note in this scale.

Can you see what I'm talking about with these pentatonic scale patterns being the same as the major? With only five of them to learn, they become fairly easy to understand.

It is where they are located in each key (major or minor) that is important to know to be able to play them correctly. When you know this, you will sound good when you execute the notes within them.

Lesson 14: Minor pentatonic scale #4

This is a great scale to master. No matter if you play it in major or minor. That is because of the way the notes line up in the box pattern. What I mean by this is that there is a natural arpeggio on this scale.

Here is minor pentatonic scale #4 starting where #3 left off at the 12th fret. Once again, the same scale as the #3 major pentatonic.

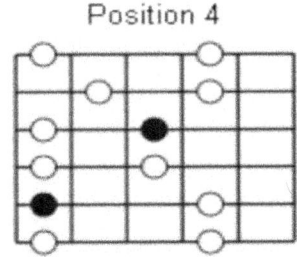

12

Notice the location of the root note A has changed once again from the last scale pattern. Make sure you go through the scale and listen to these notes. They are very important to know.

Make sure that you go through these scale patterns and know them like the back of your hand. Make sure that you can visualize their shapes and recognize the difference.

Lesson 15: Minor pentatonic scale #5

Minor pentatonic scale #5 is also a favorite of mine because it is easy to learn. The notes line up in such a way that it is also easy to visualize.

```
T|--------------------------------------15--17--|
A|-----------------------------15--17------------|
A|-----------------14--17------------------------|
B|--------15--17---------------------------------|
 |--15--17---------------------------------------|
```

Here we have the 5th minor pentatonic scale in the key of A minor at the 15th fret.

Once again we can see that it is the same as the #4 major pentatonic in C major. This is great because this just confirms our knowledge of this scale pattern.

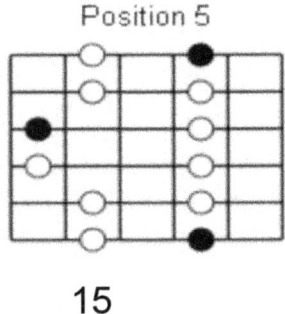

15

As before with the other minor pentatonic scale patterns, look at where the root note placement is. You want to make sure you know this because when you switch to other keys, this root note placement will stay the same.

This is great because once again, it takes out the guesswork on the root note location. Knowing where the root note is in the scale is very important. That is why I present the diagrams as well as the tabs. It gives you a visual on where these notes are located within each scale.

I highly recommend you take some time to fully understand how to read these two formats. This skill set will only enhance your ability to become a better lead guitar player, and overall better musician.

Chapter 3 summary

In this chapter we have covered some very important musical concepts. We have learned the 5 minor pentatonic scales, and also learned that they are the same shapes as the major pentatonic scales.

In the minor pentatonic scales we start with the first position (which is the fifth position in the majors) and remember that it is the most common of all the pentatonic scales. No matter if you are playing minor or major.

The reason why it's a minor scale is because it is made up of the 1, b3, 4, 5, and b7. The notes that make up the minor pentatonic scale. This goes for any key you choose to play in. Em, Bm, Gm, etc. That is what is so great about this scale.

Although you change positions of where you play it, the notes always line up in the perfect order to sound good over the key you choose to play it in. And it is for this reason that makes it such an awesome scale to use for playing guitar solos.

Minor pentatonic scale #2 is also the major pentatonic scale. This is because of the way the notes line up within the scale. We learned earlier that the major pentatonic scale is made up of the 1, 2, 3, 5, & 6, and that is what this scale is made up of.

We also learned about the major scale having a relative minor. This relative minor scale is always going to be located three frets down from the major. And if you take note, the minor pentatonic scale is located down three frets from the major.

So we can come to the conclusion that A minor is the relative minor of C major. Why? Because it is located three frets down and the notes are the same in each scale. This makes them relative. And this works with all keys.

Study these five pentatonic scale patterns. Notice how their location relates to both keys. Make sure you can play them in both C major and A minor. Also learn where the root notes are in each key.

This will help with all other major and minor keys you'll play guitar solos in. Remember, it is not just knowing the scale patterns that is important, it is knowing where to play them and how to connect them together.

Chapter 4 Guitar Solo Techniques

Lesson 16: Hammer-ons

Now that we have learned the five pentatonic scales and can play them in both C major or A minor (don't worry, I'll show you how to play them in other keys later) we want to learn how to bring them to life.

How to get them to sound like guitar solos that we hear in our favorite songs by our favorite guitar players. That is what this chapter is about. Common guitar solo techniques that will allow us to do that.

Many times I see guitar players knowing the minor pentatonic scale, but when they play it, it sounds like they are just running through notes. We want to avoid this. The first technique we will learn is the most common, hammer-ons.

Hammer-ons are when you play a note and then hammer-on to another one. This gives the notes character and keeps the scale from sounding mechanical.

Here is an example of the hammer-on and some ways to play it within the minor pentatonic scale. I'll show you these on this scale because it is most common. But once you learn the technique, be sure to try it on the other scales as well.

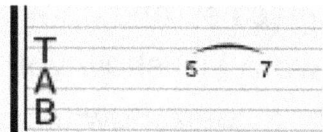

Here is a hammer-on at the 5th fret to the 7th fret on the third string. You pick the 5th fret and hammer-on (without picking) the 7th fret.

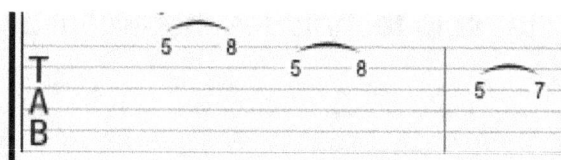

These are hammer-ons within the #1 minor scale. On the first string, second string, and third string. All at the 5th fret.

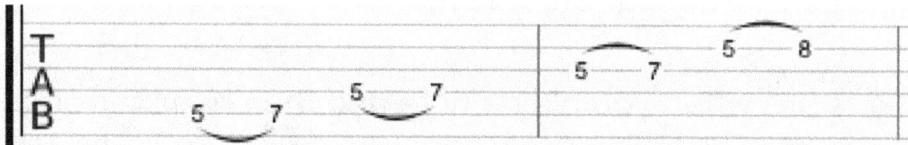

Here we have a hammer on at the 5th fret on the fifth, fourth, third, and second strings. All within minor pentatonic scale #1.

Remember that a hammer-on in the tab is indicated by an arc between the two notes. This will become more familiar as we progress with the training.

Lesson 17: Pull-offs

If a hammer-on is adding a note, then a pull-off is when you take a note away. Kind of like adding and subtracting in math. Same concept.

A pull-off is when you hold down two notes, pick one note and pull-off to the other note. Like for instance you pull-off from the 7th fret to the 5th fret on a given string.

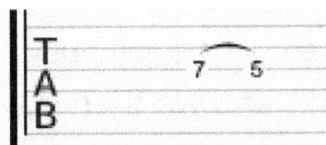

Here we have a pull-off at the 7th fret. You hold down both notes, play the note at the 7th fret and pull-off to the 5th fret on the third string.

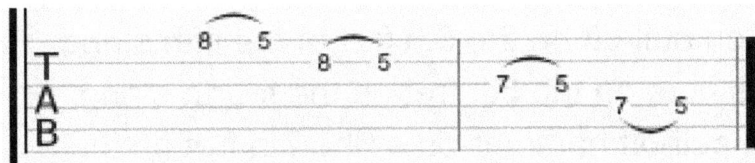

Here is a combination of pull-offs within the minor pentatonic scale. As before with the hammers-ons, except backwards. From the 8th fret to the 5th.

Once you learn how to execute the hammer-ons and pull-offs individually, you then want to work at playing them together. This is where things start to get fun and sound cool.

When doing them together, the arc that represents the hammer-ons and pull-offs will be over three numbers instead of just two.

As you can see, the arc is over all the numbers. This tells us that we hammer-on to the 7th fret from the 5th and we then do a pull-off from the 7th fret back to the fifth.

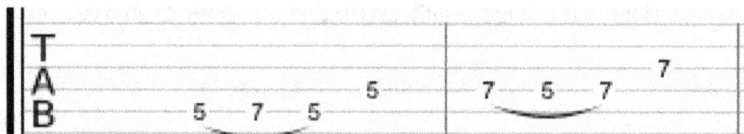

Here is a hammer-on pull-off on the 5th fret of the fifth string followed by a single note on the 5th fret on the fourth string. Then followed by a pull-off hammer-on at the 7th fret on the fourth string followed by a single note at the 7th fret on the third string.

Work on stringing these two techniques together. You'll soon see how it adds character to the notes within the scale.

Lesson 18: Bends and slides

After you get the hammer-ons and pull-offs down, you want to learn how to bend the strings within the scale. Because it adds expression to the notes that is different than the hammer-ons and pull-offs.

When it comes to bending notes, there are a few different heights of the bend that you can do. Bend up one fret, this is a half step. Or bend up two frets that is a whole step. And if you really want to get expressive, you can try a step in a half.

But for now, let's just keep it simple and bend up a little. This will give us time to see how the technique makes the note sound, and develop our finger muscles to bend notes. Not always easy, but with practice you can do it.

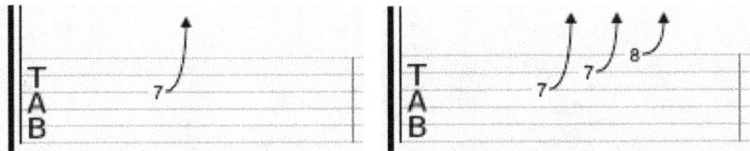

A bend is represented by a line going up. I know you're going toward the first string and it seems that it would be a bend down, but it's really a bend up. Sorry for the confusion, but I didn't design it, I just teach it.

Anyway, there are different ones you can do. But for now, just practice picking a note within the scale and bending it up like in the examples. Don't worry about how high up, just work at developing your fingers to execute the technique.

In addition to bending notes, you can also slide from note to note. This is another cool technique that allows you to give character to the notes. You simply slide from one note to the other.

Here is a slide from the fifth fret to the 7th on the third string. A slide is represented by a diagonal line that is either pointing up or down. Depending on the direction of the slide.

Here we combine the two techniques.

In the previous example, you slide up and down from the 5th fret to the 7th and then bend up the 7th note three times. All on the same string. This is called a guitar lick (we'll learn more about these later) and should be practiced daily.

Playing lead guitar is not easy and takes lots of practice. That is why the lead guitar player gets the spotlight. Make sure to focus on these techniques and how to execute them properly.

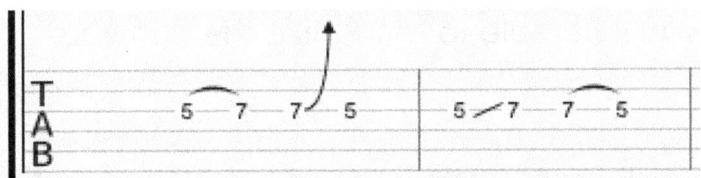

Here is an example of all the techniques learned so far. A hammer-on, bend, slide and pull-off. This is how you create guitar solos that sound interesting.

You don't just want to play the notes of the scale. You want to bend them, slide them, hammer-on to them and pull-off from them. These things will make you sound awesome!

Let's look at a few more techniques that will add cool character and expression to the pentatonic scales. Remember, it doesn't matter if you're playing in a major or minor key. These techniques will work on all five scales.

Lesson 19: Vibrato and trills

Now that we have some cool techniques down, let's look at a few more. Vibrato and trills. Vibrato is when you pick the note and vibrate it. Very much like a singer who vibrates their vocal cords.

A trill is when you play a repeated hammer-on pull-off in a fast concession. What is really neat about these techniques, is that once you learn them you'll be able to recognize them in your favorite guitar solos.

```
      ~~~~  ~~~~      ~~~~  ~~~~
T|--------------5--|----5---------|
A|--------5--------|----------5---|
B|--5--------------|--------------|
```

Vibrato is represented by a squiggly line above the note. Here we have a vibrato on a few different strings all at the 5th fret.

Pick the note and then bend it slightly up and down until you get a vibrating effect. This can be a bit difficult to get at first so don't get discouraged if it takes a few tries.

Vibrato is one of the toughest lead guitar techniques to get down for some people. So if that is you, don't worry. You'll get it. Just make sure you practice it daily.

Do so, and you will be able to make just one note sound better than most people make ten. But it will take practice. Don't overlook this.

Trills are kind of the same way in the fact that they don't come easy for everyone. The reason for this is because you need to develop strength in your finger muscles. And this takes time. But like vibrato, put in the time and you'll sound awesome.

```
       tr~         tr~
T
A                5 (7)
B      5 (7)
```

Here are a couple trills on the 5th fret of the fourth and third strings. The number in parentheses is the note you trill to. In this case the 7th note.

You just do a hemmer-on pull-off repeatedly. The trill is represented by a tr with a squiggly line after it. This is another very cool lead guitar technique that brings character to the notes.

Chapter 4 Summary

In this chapter we have learned some really cool techniques that will bring the notes in the scale to life. These techniques will make them sound like music. Like the guitar solos you hear from your favorite players.

The first technique is the hammer-on. This technique can be found in every rock guitar solo on the planet. It is a very common way to add a note to what you are playing without picking it.

The pull-off is the same thing except backwards. Instead of adding a note, you're taking one away. Hammer-ons you start with one note and hammer-on to another, with pull-offs, you start with two and take one away.

Bends are also a great way to add emotion to your guitar solos and melody lines. You strike a note and bend it up. Start with a small bend and let your fingers develop. Once they do over time, you can then bend the strings higher.

Slides are another great way to catch attention with the notes in the scales. You can strike a note and slide up or down to any fret you choose. You can slide within one scale as I have shown, or you can slide within multiple scales.

Vibrato is one of the most common techniques in all stringed instruments. Especially guitar. Work with this technique daily and see if you can develop it. Expressing a single note this way is done by many, many, great guitar players.

Once you have the hammer-ons and pull-offs down, you can then work at repeating them rapidly to create trills. Another very cool technique that catches attention when it is executed properly.

These are the fundamental concept techniques of giving expression to the scales. Any scale. As you go through learning them, listen to how they sound and try to recognize them in guitar solos that you listen to.

Learn these techniques individually, then try to put them together collectively. We will learn more about doing this later in this book. But for now, just concentrate on these basic lead guitar techniques and principles.

48

Chapter 5 When To Play The Scales

Lesson 20: Song intro

When it comes to guitar solos and melody lines, there are many different places within a song to play them. And there is no rule of right or wrong. It just depends on what is best for you and what you are trying to create.

That being said, let's start with the opening of a song. There are many songs that start a song with a guitar solo. Right out of the gate you throw out some awesome memorable melody line. A great way to catch the attention of the listener.

You can also use the scales in the intro to play a catchy guitar riff. This is very common in rock guitar. Where most of the songs are made up of some sort of guitar riff that catches the attention of the listener.

As you listen to your favorite songs, listen to this approach. Starting the song off with a guitar riff, melody line, or guitar solo to grab the listener. These are the things that make you perk up and say "ooh, that's cool."

50

Here are a couple examples of this approach to playing guitar scales at the intro of a song.

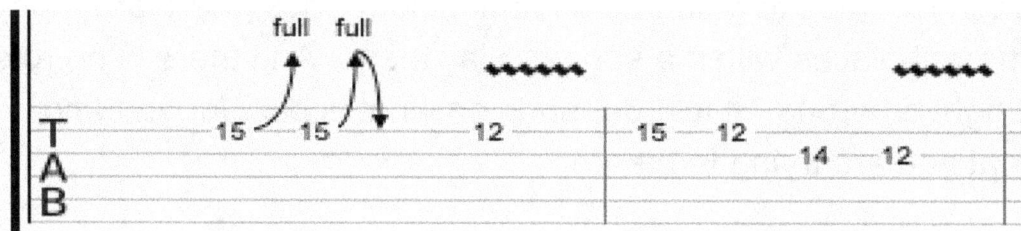

Here we have a bend up on the 15th fret followed by a bend release on the 15th fret and a vibrato on the 12th fret.

We then proceed through a few more notes in the minor pentatonic scale.

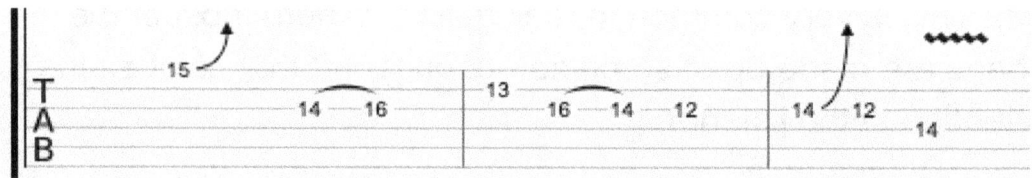

Very similar intro here, but utilizing the 16th and 14th frets as well. Also notice the added use of the hammer-on and pull-off.

Let these examples give you ideas on what you can do to create a lead guitar intro in a song.

51

Lesson 21: Song middle section

The most common place to put a guitar solo or melody line is in the middle section of a song. The reason for this is because it gives the listener a break from the back and forth of the verse and chorus part.

Aside from putting an intro guitar solo in the song, you can also put one in the middle. Or you can choose not to put a solo in the beginning and just have one in the middle.

Ideas for this are endless, but here are a few simple examples that you can learn. These are ideas that incorporate the techniques that you have learned so far.

Example #1

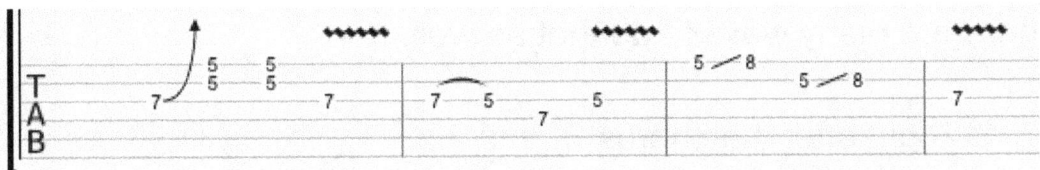

Example #2

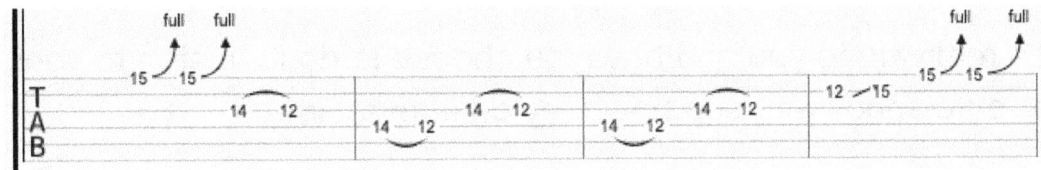

Example #3

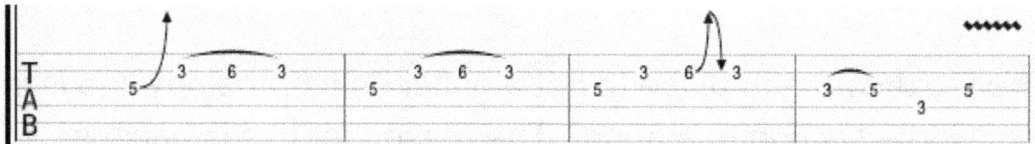

Example #4

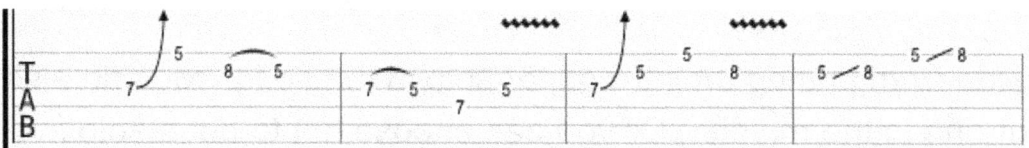

All these examples can be used as middle section guitar solos. Of course, since these are just examples you might need to make them longer, but they give you a nice place to start. Let these examples spark your imagination.

When it comes to putting guitar solo in the middle of a song there are many ways to do that as well.

1. Right after the chorus
2. Right after a bridge
3. Right after a verse

It's really up to you and how you choose to do it. Listen to your favorite songs and see how they do it to get ideas.

53

Lesson 22: Song outro

The last place you can put a guitar solo is at the end of a song. Sometimes this works in addition to a middle section solo.

Actually, you can put a guitar solo or melody line anywhere you choose, but these are the most common places within a song. As you get familiar with guitar solos and song structure, you'll see where these ideas are common.

Example #1

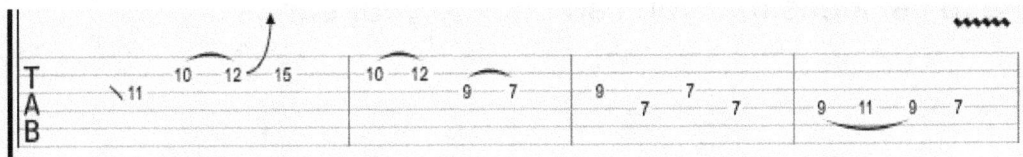

Example #2

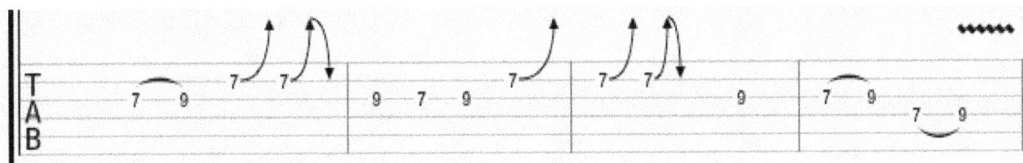

Example #3

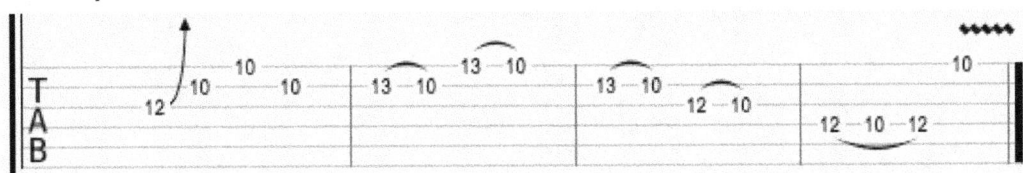

All three of these examples give you an idea of what is possible for creating outro solos. Actually, any solo idea can be used as an outro solo. Even the ones I mention in the intro and middle section.

It is really up to you and your creativity. How you choose to do it. I recommend you look at some songs with outro solos and see how they are structured. How do they begin? Where do they start? After a verse? After a chorus?

By studying popular songs that utilize this method, you'll be able to get ideas that you can put into your songs.

Lesson 23: Acapella

In my opinion, this is the funnest place to put a guitar solo. Outside of the song. This is where the lead guitar player plays a piece of music without the band or any accompanying music. Just play all by him/herself.

This can be a lot of fun. But in order to do this, you must study and practice. Only the best can do this with confidence. Very much like a singer singing without the band.

This will be a place to test your musicability as well as your stamina. As acapella soloing demands that these skills be sharp! It also shows that you are a band leader and that you can handle the spotlight being only on you.

It takes massive hours of study and practice to accomplish this. But if you put in the string time, it will allow you to build the confidence within yourself to play outside of the band and establish yourself as a leader.

Any of the solo examples that I have presented can be used for this purpose. You can also use them as ideas to create your own acapella solo.

With that being said, here are some more ideas that you can use for this purpose:

Example #1

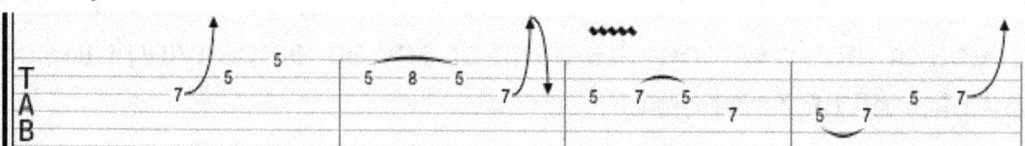

Example #2

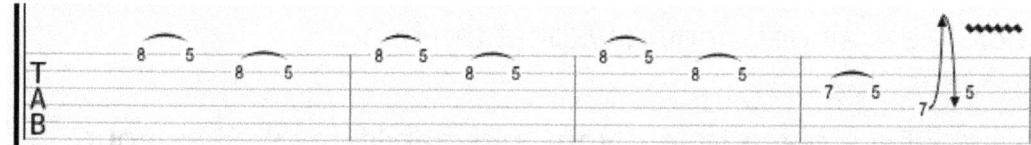

Example #3

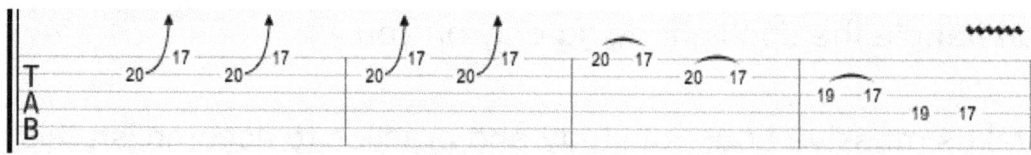

Example #4

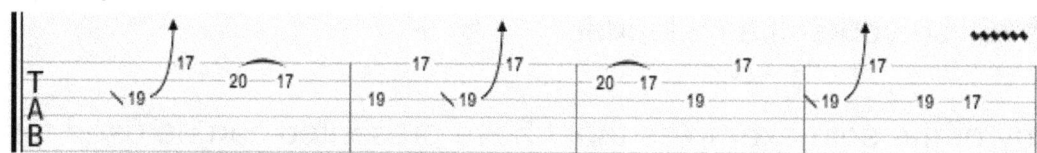

All these licks can be used individually or collectively to create an awesome acapella guitar solo.

Lesson 24: Harmonizing

Another cool way of playing guitar solos is with notes that harmonize. Harmonizing is when you play certain notes together to create a certain type of sound.

Harmonizing can also be done with two guitar players and very common with bands that have multiple guitarists.

Here is an example of how this works:

Example#1

```
-----------------------------------------8----10--
------5--7--9--------5--4-------------5--7--------
--7-----------------------5-----7-----------------
--------------------------------7--8--------------
--------------------7-----------------------------
```

This is one guitar doing single notes.

Example #2

```
----------------------------------------7----8---
------5--6--8--------5--3-------------5--6---8--10
--5---5--7--9--------5--4--4----------5--5--7-----
--7-----------------------5--5--7--7--------------
--------------------------------7--8--------------
--------------------7-----------------------------
```

Here is the same guitar line, except with a harmonized part. These are harmony chords that simulate two guitar players

.

This second example can be played by one guitarist or two. It just depends on your situation. The main thing you want to get out of this lesson is what notes are best used for this technique.

Harmonizing is usually done in thirds, fifths, sixths and octaves.

What does this mean? Let me explain.

Let's use the key of C major. C D E F G A B C

In this key we have 8 notes and we give them number values of 1-8. So, C is 1, D is 2, E is 3, etc, etc, etc.

So if we were to harmonize in thirds in the key of C major we would use the 1and 3 of the scale. These two notes would be the C and E.

If we were to harmonize in fifths, we would use the 1 and 5. These notes would be the C and G. If we wanted to harmonize in 6ths the notes would be C and A.

Make sense?

If you were going to Harmonize in octaves you would choose the C note. One in the lower octave and one in the higher octave.

These can be found on each string in certain locations and it is recommended that you learn your notes on your fretboard to quickly locate them.

Here is another example of harmonizing:

Example#3
```
                5--7--                                        5------10-----12
        5--8--                   8--7--                  5--8--     8-----10
         5--7--9                 5--4--7--4         5--      5--7
      7                             5                  7
                                       7           8
```

As you can see, this one is a bit different in the fact that you sometimes skip a string to play the notes. This is because of where they are located.

Harmonizing is a very cool effect you can do with the guitar to create solos and melody lines. You just need to know your notes so you can locate them on the fretboard.

Study this chapter and try this out in other keys. You'll see very quickly that you'll be able to come up with all kinds of cool ideas for guitar solos.

Chapter 5 Summary

In this chapter we have looked at some very important concepts when it comes to playing guitar solos. Like where to play them in a song.

In the beginning of the song is a great place to put a guitar solo. It grabs the listener right off the bat and sets the tone for the whole song.

Another place to put the guitar solo is in the middle of the song. This location is the most common. It is placed here to give the listener a break from the verse and chorus that comes before it. Placing the guitar solo here can be done in multiple ways.

You can place it right after the chorus. This is a pretty common method. Or you can place a bridge in the song and then put the guitar solo after that.

A common way of doing this is to sandwich the solo between the bridge. Meaning you create a bridge piece that is different from the verse and chorus and then play the solo, and then play the bridge again after.

You can also choose to play the guitar solo in the middle with or without a bridge and then go back to the beginning. This is another common way to structure a song.

Then there is the outro solo. Not all songs have this, but this is another cool place to put a guitar solo. This is a great way to end a song that has a "jam" feel to it.

What I mean by that is some rhythms that are created, can be played indefinitely. This can be great for solo improvisation. Especially if you have more than one lead guitar player. You can both take turns doing guitar solos.

If you do happen to find a friend who plays guitar and you both play guitar solos, you can switch off like suggested as well as harmonize.

This is where things can get real fun with two guitar players. You can create some really fun musical pieces by harmonizing. This can be done in 3rds, 5ths, 6ths, and octaves.

Give these ideas a try when creating your guitar solos. Think about different placements. Intro, middle, outro, and even harmonizing. Even if you're just one guitar player, you can do this with harmony chords.

62

Chapter 6 Where To Play The Scales

Lesson 25: Key of G major/minor

Now that we know what the scales are, some techniques to bring them to life and some good locations within a song to play them, we now want to learn where to play them within a key.

This is important to know because your songs will be written within a certain key. No matter what key it is. All songs are written in a certain key. And it is this key that will tell us where to play our guitar solos.

So if by chance you're writing a song in a certain key (like the key of G minor) you'll know where to play the solo. Or if you happen to play with someone, and they say "the song is in the key of A minor", you'll know where to play the solo there too.

In this chapter we are going to look at where to play the guitar solo in the key of G major and the key of G minor.

Before doing this we want to understand what makes up a key. A musical key like G major for instance is made up of 8 notes. The Do Re Mi that was mentioned earlier. All major keys have this sound. So it is important to know this.

A minor key is the same thing, but a few of the notes in the major key are flattened by one fret to make it a minor. In the key of G major, we will need to flatten the 3rd, 6th, and 7th notes to make it a minor key.

Let me explain further.

The key of G major consists of the notes:

```
1   2   3   4   5   6   7   8
G   A   B   C   D   E   F#  G.
Do  Re  Mi  Fa  So  La  Te  Do
```

As you can see we have 8 notes, 8 letters and they are all relative to the Do Re Mi. So we can say that the G is the 1st note, the B is the 3rd note, and the D is the 5th note. This goes for all the notes in the key or scale as it is also called.

To play a guitar solo in this key, we need to know where the G note is located on the fretboard. Well, it is actually located in multiple places on the fretboard. To make it easier, we look for it on the low E string. This location will be at the 3rd fret.

Since we learned the major pentatonic scales already, we can now come to the conclusion that we can play them here at the 3rd fret on the 6th string and be in the key of G major.

We simply start with scale pattern one and proceed forward through all five. This works because the major pentatonic scale is using the notes that come out of the G major scale. If we follow the pattern, it will sound good every time.

That is, if it is played in this position. If we were to say, play the major pentatonic scale at the 4th fret, it would not sound good in the key of G major because it would be in a different major key. Using different notes.

Some notes might work because they are in both keys, but traditionally not all of them would work. This is where most guitar players have problems when playing guitar solos. Knowing where to play within a certain key.

Now, if we look at the major pentatonic scale and we play it at the 3rd fret, the notes would line up like this:

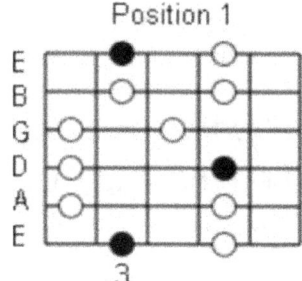

As you can see, this major pentatonic scale is played at the third fret where the G is located. Notice the other G notes located within the scale.

If you go back to when we learned them in C major, you'll see they are in the same location as those notes. This happens in all major keys and takes out the guesswork.

Can you see how cool this is? Can you see how easy it makes playing the proper notes to stay in key?

Since the first position starts at the third fret, and the second scale starts where the first one leaves off, then the second major pentatonic scale will start?

67

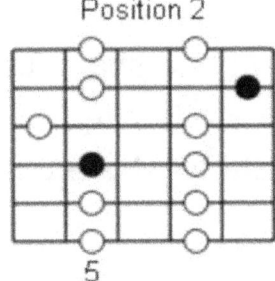

At the 5th fret. And once again, we can see where the G notes are located. Same place as in the key of C major. This is very important to remember.

The 3rd scale pattern will be located?

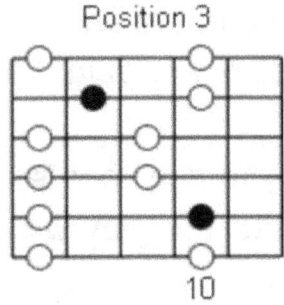

At the 7th fret. This scale pattern will span from the 7th to the 10th fret.

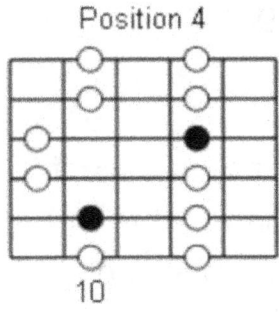

As you can see, pattern four starts at the 10th fret and spans to the 12th. Once again, notice where the G notes are located within the scale pattern. The final scale pattern starts where this one leaves off.

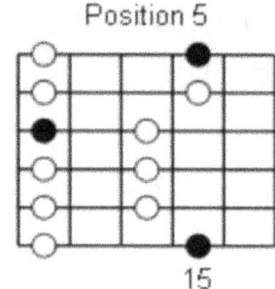

At the 12th fret. This leads us back to the G note in the second octave at the 15th fret, and the process starts all over again.

Can you see how these scales will make it easy to play in this major key? Since these notes all come from that key, they will all sound good.

So, just stay within these scales when you play and you'll be fine. Kind of like driving your car on the road. Stay on the road and it should be smooth sailing. Go up on the grass and sidewalk and it gets rough.

This also works for the minor keys. So for G minor, we want to play the minor scales. And since they are the same, this works. We just start with the fifth scale pattern in the first position.

We discussed earlier that to make a minor key, we need to flatten a few notes of that major key. The 3rd, 6th, and 7th notes.

So if we take the G major scale, G A B C D E F# G and flatten those notes, we then have G A Bb C D Eb F G. We have now flattened the 3rd, 6th, and 7th notes of the key or scale.

Now we have the 1 b3 4 5 and b7 that we can use for the key of G minor. These are the notes that are in the minor pentatonic scales played starting at the 3rd fret.

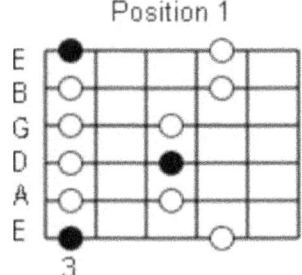

As you can see, this scale starts at the same fret. The 3rd. You are now playing in G minor and playing a G minor scale in this key.

If you look at the notes, from G to G, you'll see that you are playing the notes I mentioned earlier. The 1, b3, 4, 5 and b7 of the G major scale. That is why this minor pentatonic scale works in this key.

But it must be played at the 3rd fret in order for this to work. If you play it in a different spot the notes will change and some notes won't line up and sound good. But if you are in the right position, they will every time.

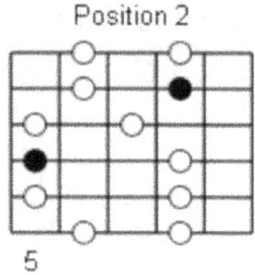

As before, the second pattern starts where the first one leaves off. At the 6th fret.

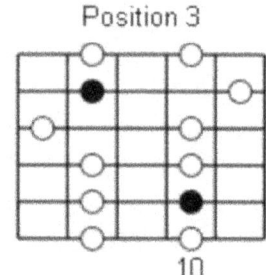

This one starts at the 8th fret. Notice where the notes are in this scale pattern.

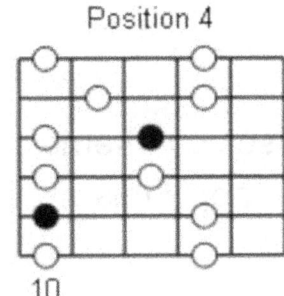

Position 4

Here the fourth pattern starts at the 10th fret. The G notes are now on the fifth and third strings.

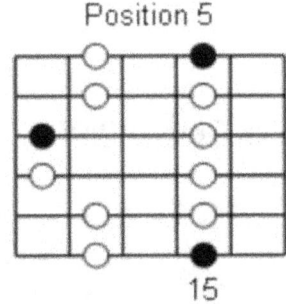

Position 5

This scale pattern in the key of G minor is located at the 13th fret. Finishes off at the 15th fret which is the G note in the second octave.

In this chapter we have gone over the pentatonic scales in both G major and G minor. Although they have the same patterns, it is where you play them that makes the difference.

Play them in the correct place and you'll strike gold every time!

Lesson 26: Key of A major/minor

Now that we understand how these pentatonic scale patterns work in the key of G major and G minor, we can apply this same philosophy to any major or minor key.

In this chapter we will look at the key of A major and A minor. We have already looked at the key of A minor when we learned the minor pentatonic scales, but we will do a review here just to make sure we fully understand how these work.

Like before, we start with our notes within the key of A major. In the key of A major you have the notes,

A B C# D E F# G# A

When we flatten the 3rd. 6th, and 7th, we get the notes of the A minor scale. A B C D E F G A. As we learned before, these are the same notes in the key of C major.

This is important to know because it tells us that we can play the A minor pentatonic scales in the key of A minor as well as in the key of C major. A Minor is the <u>natural</u> minor of A major and the <u>relative</u> minor of C major.

73

This concept works with all keys. Every major key has a natural minor (flatten the 3rd, 6th, and 7th, notes) and also has a relative minor. The relative minor will be a minor scale that has the same notes. Located 3 frets down on the fretboard.

Since we looked at the scale patterns in A minor already, let's look at them in A major.

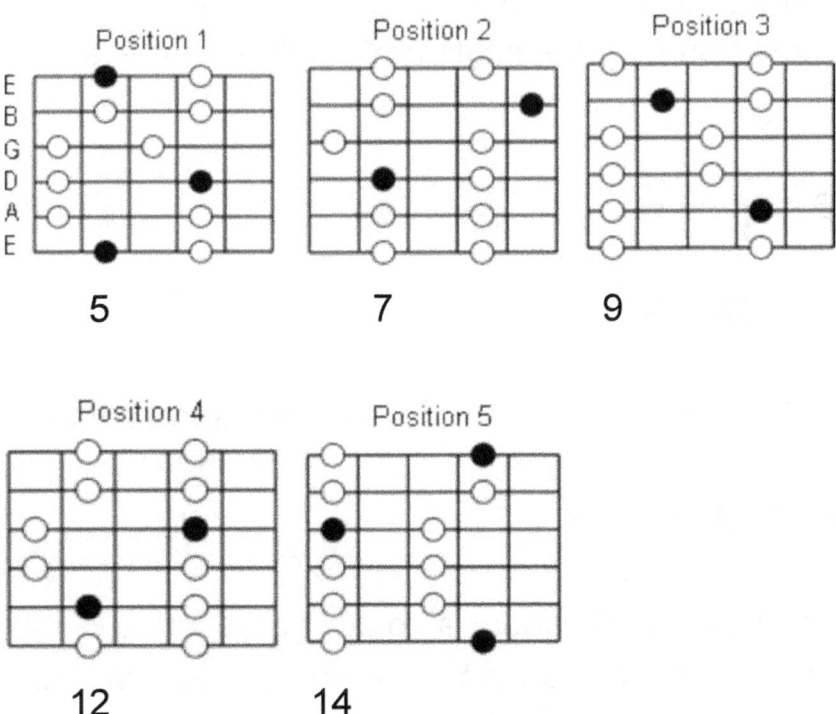

As you can see, these are the same as in the key of G major, just in the A position at the 5th fret. Play these here at these frets and you'll stay in key every time.

Lesson 27: Key of B major/minor

Same thing goes with the key of B major and B minor. We can play the major pentatonics in the key of B major, or we can play the minor pentatonics in the key of B minor.

And "technically" you can play the minor scales in the major key and vica versa because they work with both keys. It just depends on where you play the scale pattern that makes all the difference.

The notes of B major are:

B C# D# E F# G# A# B

Flatten the 3rd, 6th, and 7th, notes to make the natural minor:

B C# D E F# G A B

B major has 5 sharps and B minor has only two because of the notes we flattened. This tells us that if we come across a major key that only has two sharps, the B minor will be it's relative minor.

Here are the B major pentatonic scales:

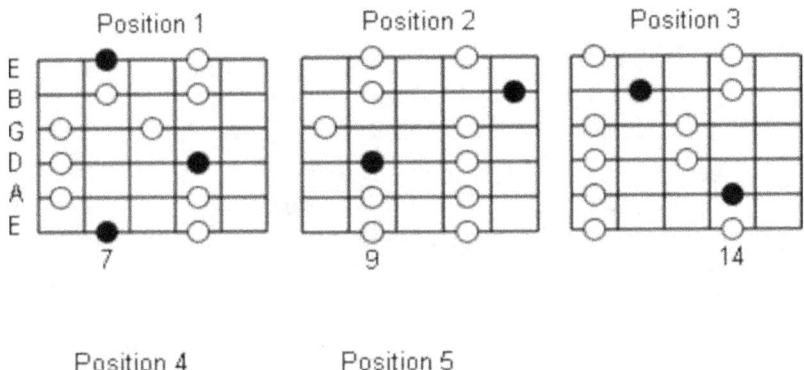

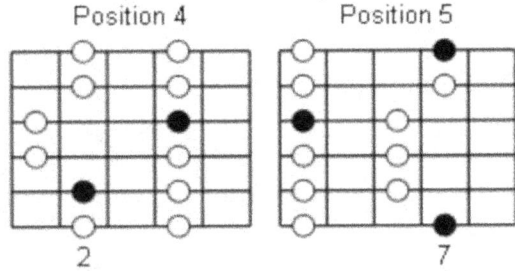

Look at where these scales start? They start at the 7th fret. This is the B note on the sixth string. If we play these major pentatonic scales here, we can be sure that we will sound good over any chord progression in the key of B major.

Here are the B minor pentatonic scales:

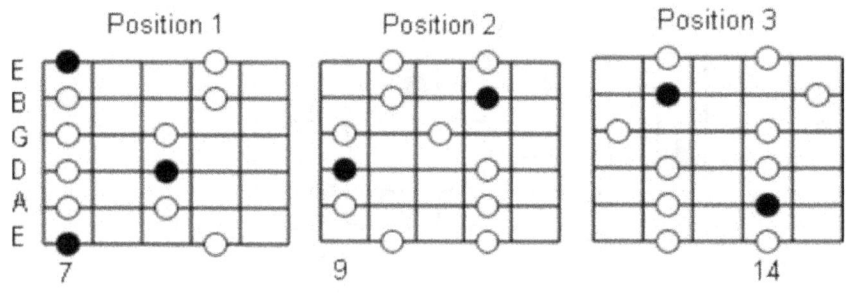

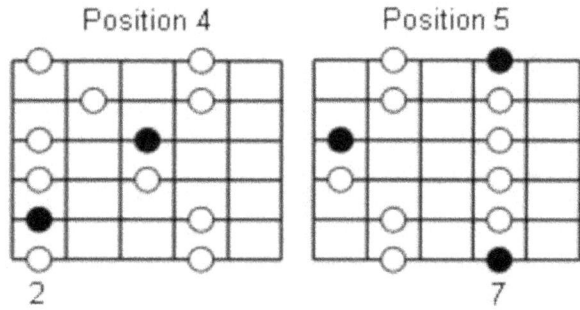

Once again, the scale patterns start at the 7th fret just like the major pentatonic scales. The only difference is that we would be playing these in B minor, and they will work over any chord progression in this key.

Notice that the B notes within the scale patterns are in the same location as in the G and A minor scales. Different from the major, because we're playing in a minor key, but same as the other minor keys.

Lesson 28: Key of D major/minor

As with the other keys that we have studied so far, this concept works the same with the keys of D major and D minor.

Here are the scale patterns for the key of D major:

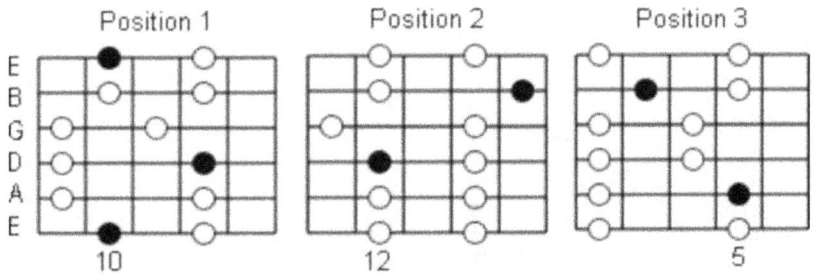

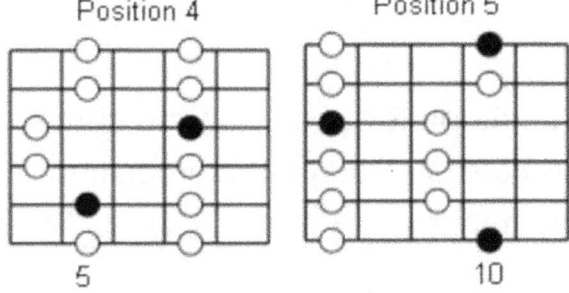

Notice that these scale patterns are in the same exact order as the other major keys but start on a different fret. They start at the 10th fret because that is where the D note is located.

Here are the scale patterns for the key of D minor:

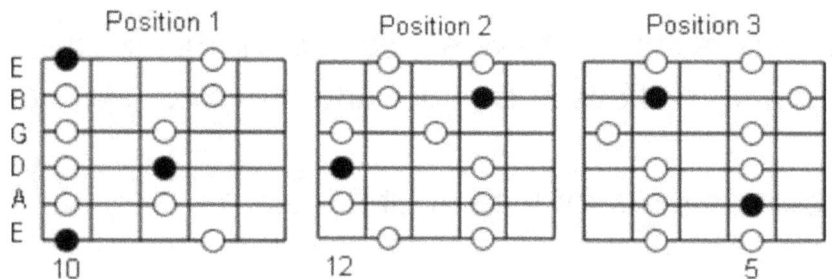

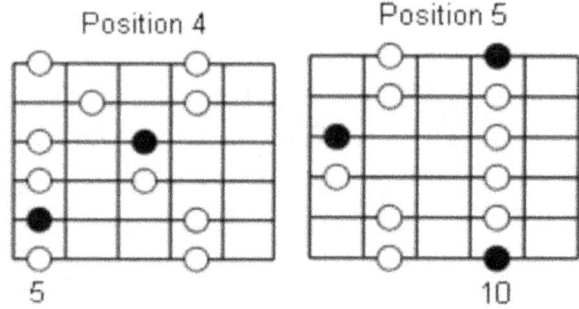

Notice once again, that these scale patterns start at the same location as the D major scale patterns. You just use position 5 of the major as position 1 of the minor.

Also, the notes for D major are: D E F# G A B C# D.

The notes for D minor are: D E F G A Bb C D

Here we can see that the D major scale is the relative major to the key of B minor. Why? Same notes.

79

Lesson 29: Key of E major/minor

The keys of E major and E minor are similar, they just have different notes.

Notes of E major: E F# G# A B C# D# E

Notes of E minor: E F# G A B C D E

E major scale patterns:

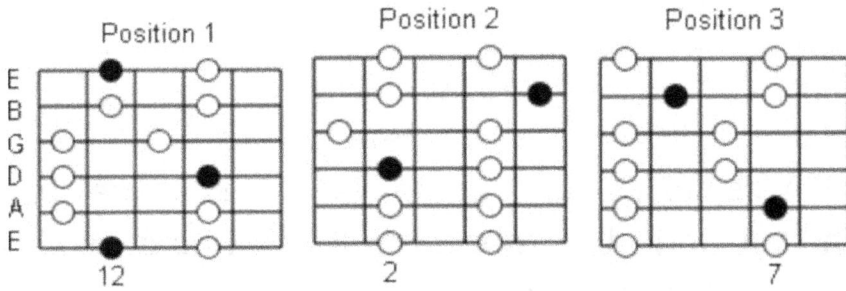

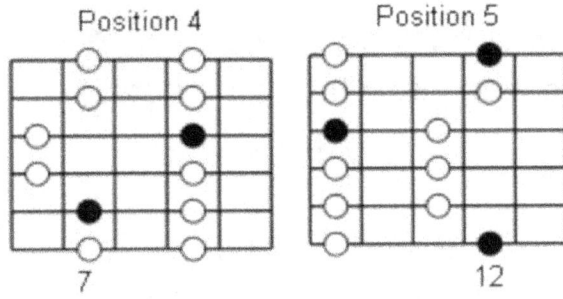

Here are the scale patterns in the key of E minor:

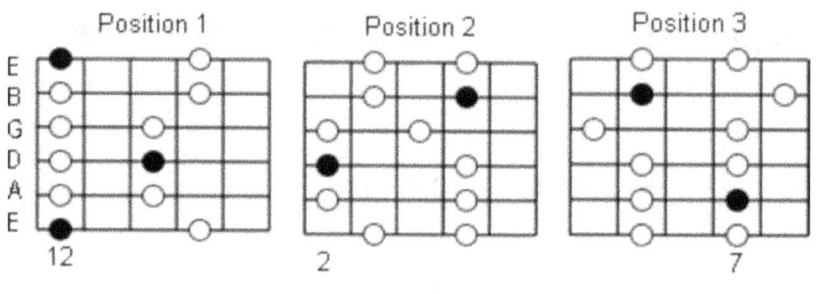

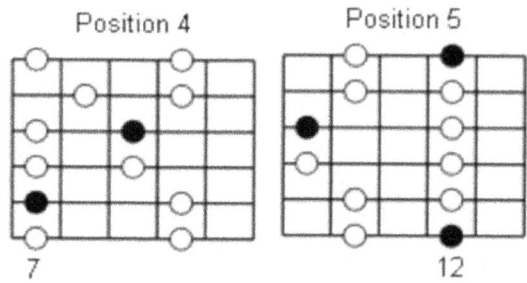

Look at where these scales start. Same place as in the key of E major. At the 12th fret. This is because that is where the E note is located on the sixth string.

Also notice that the key of E minor has an F sharp. This tells us that it is the relative minor (because it has the same notes) of the G major.

So, we can play these minor scales in both E minor, or G major. This is very important to know and should be committed to memory.

Chapter 6 Summary

In this chapter, we have looked at the major and minor pentatonic scales in 5 different keys. I chose these specific keys because they are most common when playing guitar and you should know them well.

You should also pay attention to the notes within the keys that I have presented and remember them. Also remember that if you flatten the 3rd, 6th, and 7th notes of any major key, you create the <u>natural</u> minor key.

Notice I said natural and not relative. There is a difference. The <u>relative</u> minor is a minor key that is made up of the same notes as it's relative major key. Such as in G major and E minor, or C major and A minor.

Also, notice that the scale patterns start in the same place for both major and minor keys. It is just which one of the five that you start on that makes the difference. Play them out of place and the notes won't match.

Play them in the proper place and they will every time. That is why these pentatonic scales are so popular. The notes line up in such a way that you don't even have to think about it. If you're in the right place you'll always be in key.

Remember that there are only five patterns to learn. The reason why only five is because that is how many notes are in the pentatonic scales. 1, 2, 3, 5, and 6 for the major pentatonic scale. And 1, b3, 4, 5, and b7 for the minor pentatonic scale.

If you go through the notes in these scale patterns, you will see that they are made up of these notes. This goes for any major or minor key you choose to play them in. This is the science part of music.

Another thing is to learn each pattern individually. One mistake that baffles guitar students in the beginning is when the scales are all presented together like this.

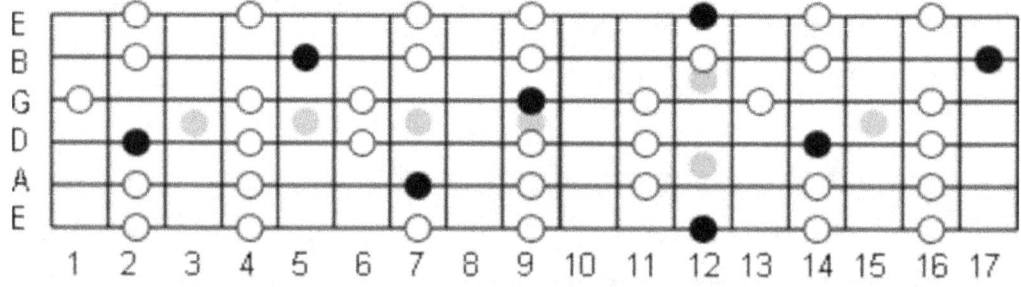

This can be too much, and a bit confusing. So don't do this until you fully understand the scales individually. Then a diagram like this will make more sense.

Chapter 7 Learning From Recordings

Lesson 30: Ear training

One thing that I highly recommend you practice when learning to understand and create guitar solos, is to learn from your favorite guitar players. This is done by listening and learning from their recordings.

I have met many guitar players and students who don't do this and time and time again I have seen that it has hindered their performance. If you're going to be serious about your learning, you want to make sure you don't hinder your education.

This also helps develop a very important part of playing guitar, ear training. Ear training is not always easy to do, but is an essential part of your learning. So in this lesson I will show you some simple techniques to help you with this vital skill.

Practice these concepts daily and I guarantee you will see progress in your ability to hear and decipher notes.

Ear training is what allows you to pick out notes by just listening to them. This skill is what allows you to get your creative ideas out of your mind and on to the guitar fretboard. Without this skill developed, your musical ideas will be crippled.

1. <u>Learn your major scale:</u>

The reason for this is because everything (as we have learned in this training so far) comes from the major scale. The Do Re Mi. All keys and scales major, minor, etc, come from this.

The more you learn this in every key, the better. The best way to learn it is to go through the major scale in every key and listen to the Do Re Mi in each one. This will help your ear get familiar with the notes that are in the key.

2. <u>Learn basic theory:</u>

I say basic because theory can go on forever. It never stops. If you'd like to go beyond the basics, great! That can only help you to get better. But at least get the basics down. How to form your basic majors, minors, augmented, diminished, etc.

This will provide the foundation that you can build on for years to come. I say years to come because there is no end to chords and scales. You can build a musical skyscraper with chords and scales.

3. <u>Learn note intervals:</u>

This is the distance between notes. Notes can either be a fret apart (a half step) or they can be two frets apart (a whole step) or they can be three frets apart (a step in a half) or possibly even four frets apart. This is two whole steps.

By being able to hear these intervals, you'll be able to pick out melodies a lot faster and decipher if chords are major or minor. As well as help you to improvise. We will go over this concept more, later in this training

4. <u>Sing the notes of a scale:</u>

Scales are created by certain intervals of the notes within the key. As we have been studying in this training. What you want to do is take one of the keys that you have learned (say G major) and play the notes on your guitar.

Then play the first note and see if you can match the pitch of the second note with your voice. Either hum the note or sing it. The objective is to be able to "hear" the pitch of the note and match it with your voice.

Do this with all the notes in all 10 (major and minor) keys that you have learned in this book. I guarantee you, that if you go through them as I suggest, it will help train your ear to hear the notes.

5. <u>Tune your guitar with a tuning fork or pitch pipe:</u>

This is a great way to train your ear to hear notes. In today's society we use electronic tuners to tune our guitars, but tuning with a tuning fork is the way it used to be done. This is still relevant today, but you don't see it as much.

Tuning with an electronic tuner is more convenient and more accurate so that is how most people tune nowadays. But as an ear training exercise, I recommend trying to tune with a tuning fork or pitch pipe.

This will force your ear to find the right pitch. Especially with a tuning fork that will give you one pitch and then you tune to that. A pitch pipe will give you all six strings. This can help you out even more. Either way, it will help develop your ear.

Practice these exercises and I guarantee that you will see improvement in hearing the notes on the guitar. It takes time though so be patient and practice daily.

Lesson 31: Practice habits

If you are going to learn from recordings, you need to develop good solid practice habits. The reason for this is because learning this way is not easy. But if you apply yourself, you will learn a wealth of information that most guitarists miss.

Solid practice habits are essential in your learning even if you don't learn from recordings as a good solid practice routine will help you to progress faster and see better results. This is why practice habits are so important.

Here are some basic practice habits to develop for maximum improvement in your guitar playing.

1. <u>Design a practice space:</u>

This is very important because it allows the mind to focus and tells it that when you get to this place, it is time to learn guitar.

Do not overlook this. It is very much like going to school or work or even your bedroom. You are directing your mind that when you get to a certain place, it is time to do something.

2. <u>Practice at the same time every time:</u>

This is also very important in getting the mind to focus. That is why you do certain things in your life at certain times. Like when you go to work, school, eat dinner, etc. It gets the mind trained. Train the mind and the body will follow.

3. <u>Focus on the fundamentals:</u>

This is something I see a lot of guitar students skip over. They think it's easy and boring and move on to more interesting concepts. But what happens later on is that they run into a hurdle and can't get over it because they didn't learn a fundamental skill. Like say, how to jump.

Just like in sports. When players get off their game, what does their coach tell them? They tell them "go back to doing the fundamentals." The same is true for music. Practice the fundamentals and you'll soar when others struggle.

4. <u>Start off slow and let progression develop:</u>

Give yourself time to develop. Your brain, and muscles need time to fully understand what it is you are trying to accomplish. So start slow. If you go too fast you'll miss things and develop bad habits that will be hard to correct later on.

5. <u>Work on what you know and what you don't know:</u>

A big mistake I see many guitar players do is only work on things they are good at. This is understandable because it gives a sense of accomplishment. But this can be false if it is the only thing worked on.

In order to progress you must step out of your comfort zone and work on things that you are not good at. You want to work on both. And it is in learning what you don't know where you'll see the best results.

6. <u>Finger exercises and hand warm ups:</u>

This is very important as well for your motor skill development. When playing the guitar, you are going to be putting your hands and fingers in weird positions. So you want to get them in shape, and keep them in shape.

This is done through finger exercises and hand warm ups. If you practice these daily before anything else, your hands and fingers will stay in shape and perform efficiently.

7. **Music theory and fretboard logic:**

Knowing where the notes are located on the fretboard and how they work together to form chords and scales will help you to develop an appreciation for the instrument you play and the language of music.

Remember, music is a language and just like any other language you want to learn how to read it, write it, and speak it. Do this and you will be ahead of 99% of guitar players.

8. **Chords, timing, and rhythm:**

Chords, timing and rhythm are the foundation of guitar playing. As a guitarist you will be creating rhythms. This will be done with guitar chords, (sometimes melody) and the timing you play those chords in will be crucial.

I have met many guitar players who skip this and their timing is something to be desired. That is why it is vitally important to work on developing this. Especially if you want to play with other musicians in the future.

Do all these things along with working on your guitar solos and you will be a well rounded musician. This development takes time, but if you are consistent with your learning, you'll come out a winner.

Lesson 32: Looping the song.

When it comes to learning solos from recordings, you'll want to use some sort of looper. This can be done in several ways. Nowadays a looping pedal is really popular.

When I was younger, before the internet, I used what is called a CD trainer. This was when CD's were all the rage. Before that it was a tape player. They really helped to capture certain parts of the song or solo and make them easier to learn.

Now you can get software that allows you to slow down the music as well as loop it. This helps with real fast passages in rhythms and solos. You can slow down the music and figure out exactly what is being played.

By learning a song from the recording, you are developing a very important skill set that all great musicians must possess. Discipline! Learning in this fashion develops this tremendously.

I highly recommend you practice this method. It will teach you many lessons at once. Lessons like, how to listen to other instruments, where you are in the music ensemble and how to improve your timing and ear training.

Lesson 33: Listening for effects

This is a very important skill to develop. It gives you insight into how certain sounds are created. As well as how effects can be used within a song. This is a great way to get ideas for when time comes to create your own songs.

Listening and working with recordings is a great way to leap forward in your playing. It will help develop your ear to not only recognize notes, but also guitar tone.

Each guitar player's sound is a bit different and by listening intently working with recordings, you'll hear how tone is created. You'll get ideas on how you might improve your guitar tone.

And believe me, this can sometimes be a lifelong study. You learn about how effects can alter the natural guitar signal. At what times are best to do this, and how it affects the dynamics of emotional content.

Guitar tone and effects are very important to a guitar player. No matter what style of music you play. Especially to a lead guitar player who specializes in playing guitar solos. Someone very much like yourself.

Let's look at some common guitar pedals.

Lesson 34: Common Guitar Pedals

One thing that makes playing rock guitar cool, is the use of guitar effects. These are usually done with guitar pedals operated by your feet. Once you learn this your guitar tone will never be the same.

There are many, many, guitar effects that can be used. But for the simplicity of this training, I'll keep it to the most common ones that are used by most guitar players.

1. <u>Overdrive/distortion:</u>

This is the most common effects pedal that is used by most guitar players. This effect changes the natural tone of the guitar to an overdrive or distortion sound. Listen to this as you learn songs and solos from recordings. This will need to be duplicated the best you can with your guitar.

2. <u>Reverb:</u>

This is probably the second most common effect that a guitar player uses in their tone. It gives a bit of a natural reverberation that adds ambiance and space to the guitar tone. Listen to this effect as it is very popular in songs and solos.

3. Wah wah:

This is probably the third most popular effect used by guitar players. The infamous wah pedal. This pedal became popular in the sixties and has stayed popular throughout the years. When you hear this effect, you'll know it and want to get one.

4. Delay:

This is a very cool effect that allows you to create an echo effect. A delayed response that can be controlled in multiple ways. This effect can make your guitar solos sound like they are from outer space!

5. Chorus:

This is also a great effect that can produce a watery type of sound. Great for arpeggiating chords in rhythm as well as for playing guitar solos.

6. Flanger:

Another cool effect that you sometimes hear in songs. This effect can give you the sound of a jet airplane taking off. It can also give you a slight delay sound that sounds a bit out of phase with the original guitar signal. Very cool effect.

7. <u>Tremolo:</u>

This is an effect that has been popular with guitar for many years. This effect has been used on many songs in the sixties and seventies. It produces a vibrating rhythmic change in pitch as well as volume output.

8. <u>Phaser:</u>

This is another pedal that has been used by a lot of guitar players in songs. Both for rhythm and guitar solos. This is done by creating a sweeping effect to the original guitar signal.

9. <u>Whammy bar:</u>

This is a great effect that can be used to lower and raise the pitch of a note. This comes standard on a strat style guitar, but if you don't have one you can use a whammy effect pedal to do the trick. A very cool effect to listen for.

There are many more guitar effects that can be used in songs, but these are the most popular. I recommend you get familiar with how they sound. This will give you insight on what you can do when creating your own guitar tone.

Chapter 7 Summary

This chapter has covered many important topics that will be essential to your development as a guitar player. As well as a lead guitarist who specializes in playing guitar solos.

Ear training is one of the most vital skills to learn. How to hear notes, and tell the distance between them. The pentatonic scales are a great place to practice this. Work on knowing the note intervals on each string within each scale pattern.

This can be done through solid practice habits. These must be developed for efficient results. Every great guitar player has developed great practice habits. Focus on the ideas that I have presented.

Be consistent. Find a place to study. Practice what you have difficulty with most. Don't be afraid to step out of your comfort zone. Be patient with your development. Remember, you are learning a new language that is both mental and physical.

Don't forget about theory. Start with the basics. Take it one step at a time, and eventually it will start to make sense.

Looping is an essential tool to work with when learning to play guitar solos from recordings. It can help you to get a part down faster by going over it multiple times. A must when you're trying to play faster guitar solos.

Looping a rhythm track you've created can also be fun to solo over. And since it loops the section of music, it gives you a chance to focus on creative ideas, or the discipline of getting something down note-for-note.

This also helps you to get familiar with the guitar tones that most guitar players use. Many guitar players use guitar effects and it is important to develop your ear for listening to these in the song you're studying.

Not only that, but they give you ideas on what effects you can use in your songs. As well as how to use them.

In this chapter I have given you a list of some of the most popular guitar effects pedals used in songs. Effects such as overdrive, reverb, wah wah, delay, chorus, etc. And don't forget that you can also get a looper pedal to help with looping music to learn it better.

Study all these and develop your own awesome guitar tone.

98

Chapter 8: Improvising

Lesson 35: Guitar licks

A very important aspect of playing guitar solos is being able to improvise. This can only be developed through study and practice on a daily basis. The best way to get started is by learning to play guitar licks.

Guitar licks are when you put the concepts you learned earlier into segments of musical paragraphs. This is called phrasing. These are the hammer-ons, pull-offs, bends, slides, etc.

Guitar solos are made up of guitar licks. You've learned some of these already so you should have a leg up on this lesson, but you can never have too many. Remember, these are what you'll use to create your musical masterpiece.

Linking these concepts together to create something pleasant to the ear is the key. Now that you know what scales to play, and where to play them to stay in key, let's look at more concepts to bring the scales to life.

100

Here are a few guitar licks within the scales that you have learned in this book. Practice them daily. Make sure that you can identify what scale pattern you are playing, and in what key you are playing it in.

Example #1

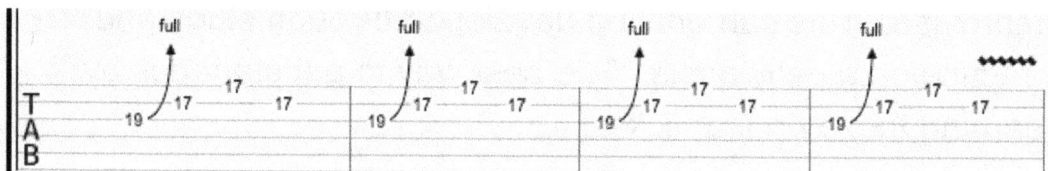

Example #2

Example #3

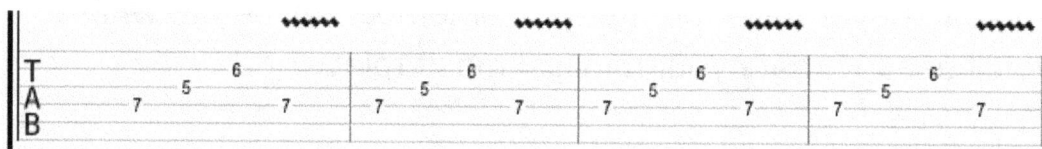

Example #4

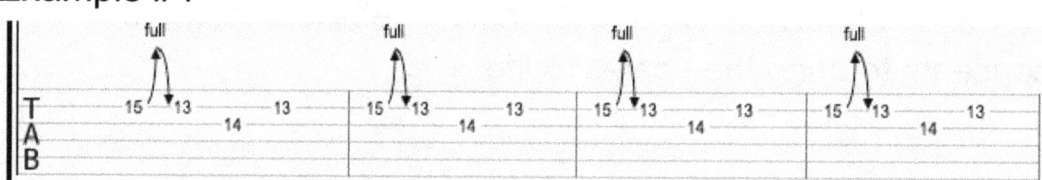

Example #5

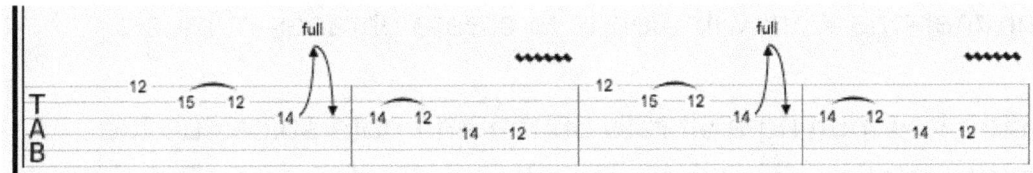

Example #6

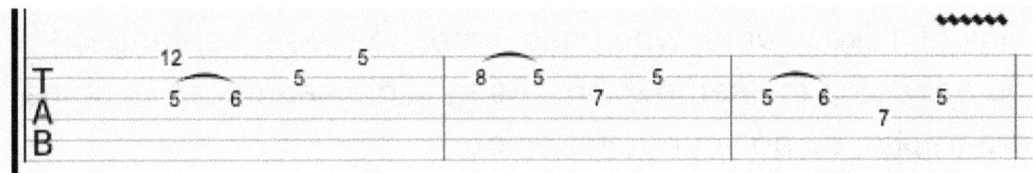

Example #7

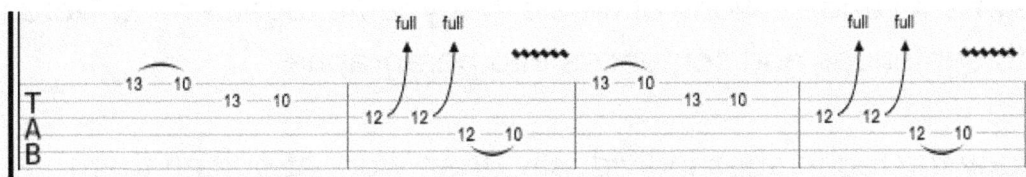

Example #8

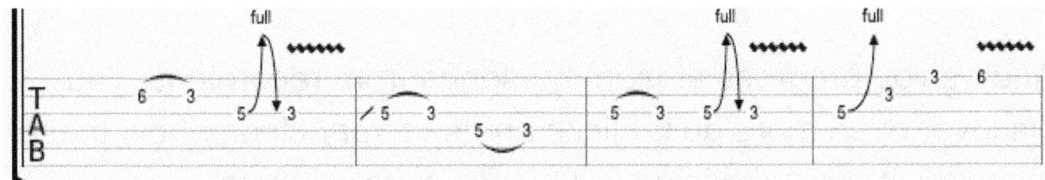

When it comes to guitar licks, they are endless. These should give you a good start on how to construct them, and how to create some of your own.

Look over these examples thoroughly. Play them and see how the techniques work well with each other. Notice how licks like hammer-ons work with bends to create phrases of music.

Listen how putting a vibrato on the end note spices up the phrase. Notice how these are little bits and pieces of music that you splice together.

Think of it like a writer who uses words to create sentences. You are doing the same thing. As multiple sentences become paragraphs, so do your guitar solos.

Try to relate guitar licks in this fashion. Look at them as segments and sections of music that you tie together like words into sentences and sentences into paragraphs.

Study the techniques individually, then work at putting them together as in the examples that I have provided. If you go over these enough, you'll see that they will become second nature.

And as you progress at learning songs from recordings, you discover even more guitar licks and see very clearly how these techniques are used by your favorite guitar players.

Lesson 36: Transposing

Once you get down what you are doing in one key (like A minor for instance) you can then work at transposing. This is where you can change the key of music to make it easier to play.

Each key is in a different pitch. And it is this pitch that gives it the character that it represents. The key of C major has a different character than the key of G major because of the pitch that the notes in it create.

The key of E minor is going to have a different character quality than B major because of its pitch. This is why the notes in each key are different. It is also why the pentatonic scales work so well in any key you choose to play them in.

By developing your ear and recognizing where your notes are located on the fretboard, over time, you'll be able to transpose into different keys and explore more of the fretboard. This will give you insight into how different keys sound.

Remember about the relative major/minor keys? These would be a great place to start transposing. Play in the major key, then transpose into the relative minor. Over time, you'll be able to modulate between different keys easily.

Lesson 37: Playing arpeggios

Arpeggios are another cool thing to use when creating guitar solos. The reason for this is that it can create a fast flowing melody line that catches attention.

An arpeggio is when you play the notes individually within a chord. A sweep picking arpeggio is like playing all the notes in the same time frame as one. Hence the term sweep picking.

Arpeggios can be used in multiple applications. What makes them work so well is they can be pulled right out of a scale pattern. Just like arpeggiating a chord. Same principle.

These can be created in both major and minor. You just need to know how to locate them. Another reason why it is beneficial to know your notes. This will allow you to locate chords within the scale patterns as well as create the arpeggios.

The best place to start with an arpeggio is in the 4th minor pentatonic scale pattern. Or the third of the major pentatonic. Remember, they are the same pattern, it just depends on where you play it that determines whether it's a major or minor.

Here is an example of an arpeggio in this scale pattern:

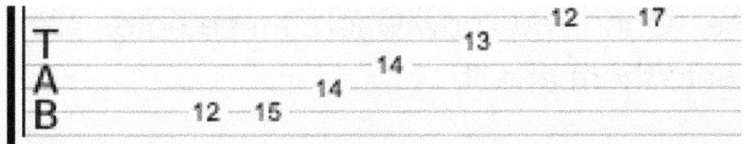

Here is the 4th pentatonic pattern in A minor:

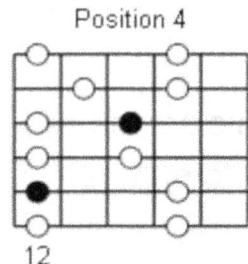

Can you see how these notes come out of this scale pattern? If you look closely, you can see that it starts on an A note at the 12th fret and ends on an A note at the 17th fret within the next scale pattern.

Here is another arpeggio out of the pentatonic scale pattern:

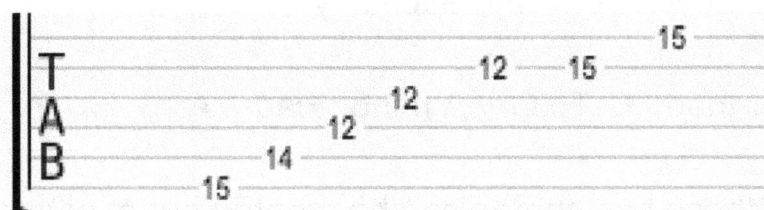

This starts and ends on a G note.

To play an arpeggio within a certain key like A minor, you want to play the notes within an A minor chord. Same thing goes with major arpeggios. Once you know where these notes are located, you can create them at will.

If you are playing the major pentatonic scale in the key of C major, you just need to find the notes that are in the C major chord (C E G) within the scale pattern and create an arpeggio out of them.

This will enhance your knowledge of the pentatonic scales as well as chord theory, note location and guitar solo creation.

Remember, arpeggios are just notes of chords played separately. This works with scales, because chords can be found in scales. Especially the pentatonic scales. So by knowing this you can find arpeggios.

Also, remember the relative major/ minor theory. Since the notes of the two keys are the same, you can create arpeggios out of the chords that will work with each key.

<u>Example:</u> C major triad: C E G.   A minor triad: A C E.

Can you see how these two chords can be created out of either the key of C major, or the key of A minor?

Lesson 38: Alternate and tremolo picking

One thing that you want to master when it comes to playing guitar solos, is alternate and tremolo picking. These are the two things that give you the ability to play fast.

Not only that, but they also allow you to play certain note passages more accurately. Certain guitar solos require this technique. You will not be able to execute it properly by just down picking. You'll have to master alternate picking.

This is where one note is picked down and the next note is picked up. Creating an alternate picking style. Here are some examples to work with in the pentatonic scales.

Example #1

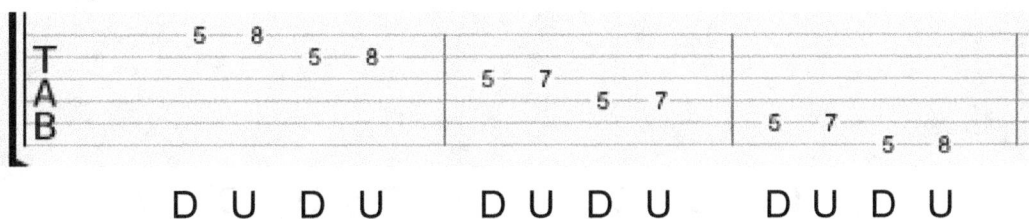

D U D U   D U D U   D U D U

Example #2

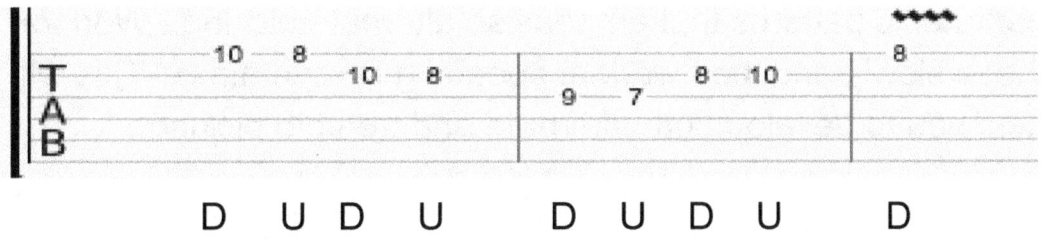

D U D U   D U D U   D

Example #3

Example #4

Example #5

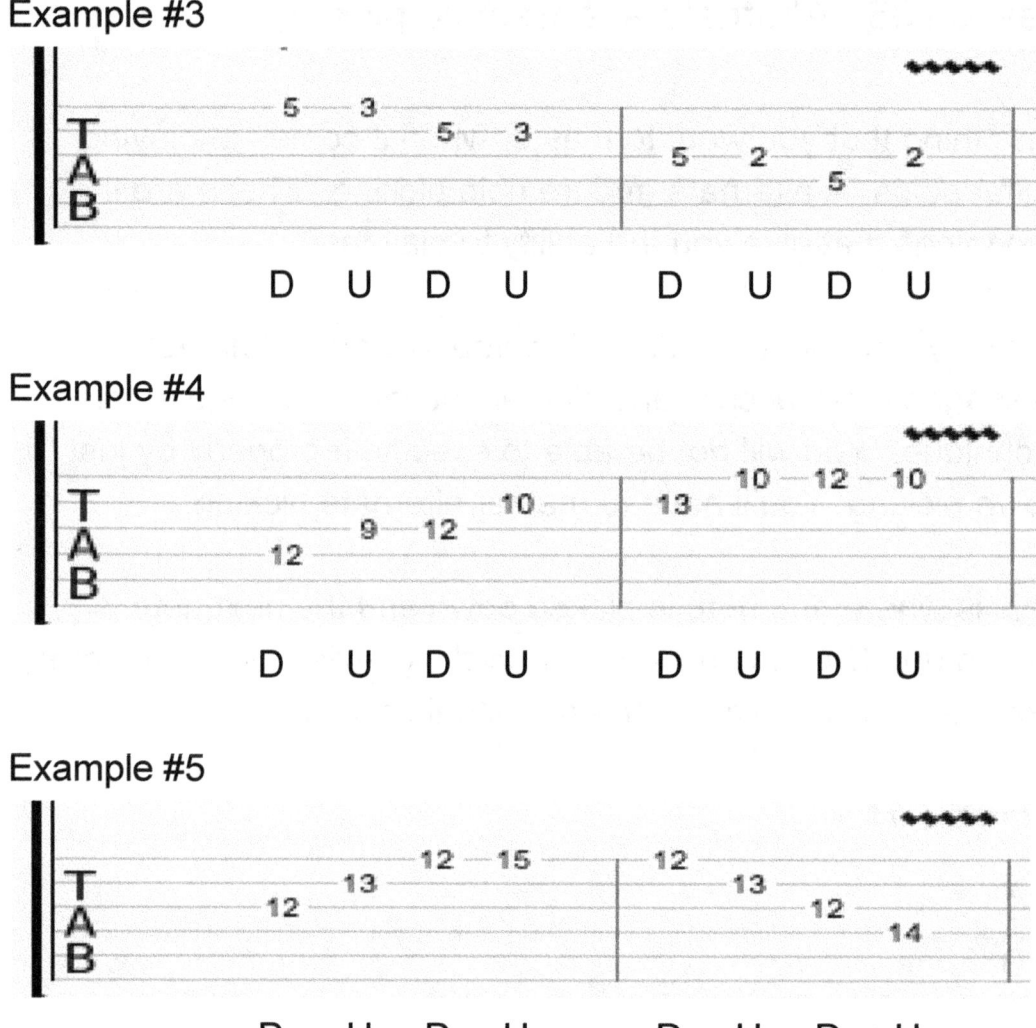

I have presented you with 5 examples of exercises within the pentatonic patterns that emphasise alternate picking. Work on these slowly and then work at speeding up over time. This will help you to develop both alternate and tremolo picking.

Lesson 39: Progressions to solo over

Here we come to the last lesson in the book. Progressions to solo over. This is probably the most important lesson in this training because we will be soloing over guitar chords. And this is where the rubber meets the road so to speak.

This is where we can play in different keys like the ones we learned in earlier lessons. C major, A minor, G major, E minor etc. By playing guitar solos over chord progressions in these keys, we really see how all this technical information works.

Knowing how to play the pentatonic scales is one thing. Where to play them is another. And how to bring them to life is still another. But the most important part is to be confident that you can play them in any key you choose to.

That way if you play with a friend or someone you meet and they say they have a song in the key of G major, you'll feel confident that you'll know where to play and it will sound great!

Of course that is if you have done your homework. If you have thoroughly studied the lessons in this book and practiced them until you know them like the back of your hand. This last lesson will help build the confidence needed.

The best place to start playing guitar solos is over the 12 bar progression. This is common in the blues and is often referred to as the 12 bar blues. But it has actually been used in other music styles like Pop, Rock, Country, and Jazz.

This is a simple three chord progression that is used in hundreds of songs. It consists of the 1, 4, and 5 of the key it's taken out of. For example in the key of C major, this would be C (1) F (4) and G (5). This works in all keys.

Here is an example of 12 bar blues in A

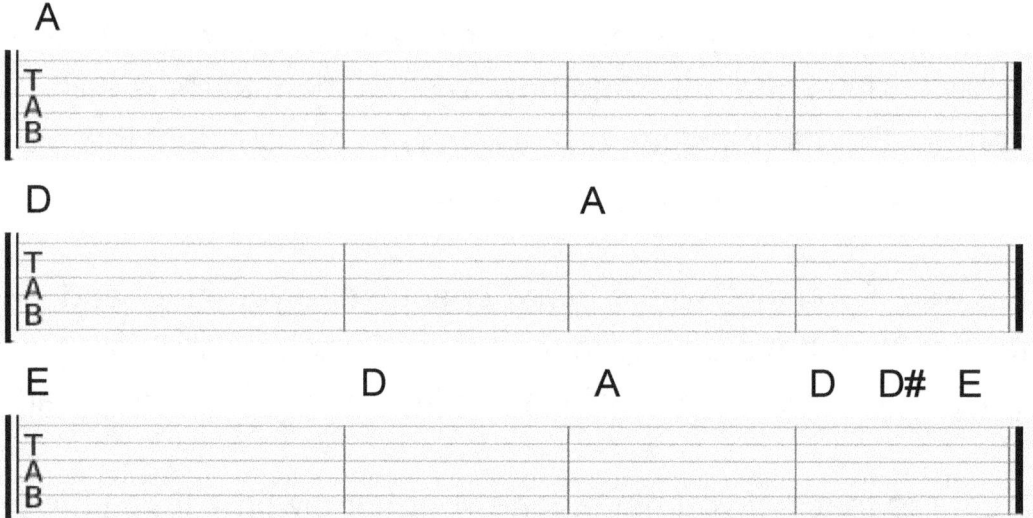

If you look at the example, it is over 12 measures and in the last measure we have what is called a turn around. This is where you put yourself in position to start the progression over.

There are many different ways to play the 12 bar progression and you will often see it presented in many different ways in other books. But the basic foundation of the progression are always the 1,4,5 chords of the key it is played in.

I have presented in A to keep it simple and easy to learn. But once you get it down in this key, transpose (move) it to other keys. Try it in B, G, E, D, etc. This will give you a better understanding of the guitar fretboard.

Not only that, but it will give a better understanding of guitar chords and how to put them together to create chord progressions. Remember, to be a good lead guitar player you must be a good rhythm guitar player.

The reason for this is because chords are what you will be soloing over and you need to know where your place is within the progression.

What's great about playing guitar solos is it gives you a chance to go off into no man's land of creativity. The scales give you the road map of where to travel and your understanding of guitar chords will let you know where to enter and exit.

Many songs you hear on the radio only have three or four chords in them. So with that being said, let's look at some easy three and four chord progressions you can play and solo over.

Example #1

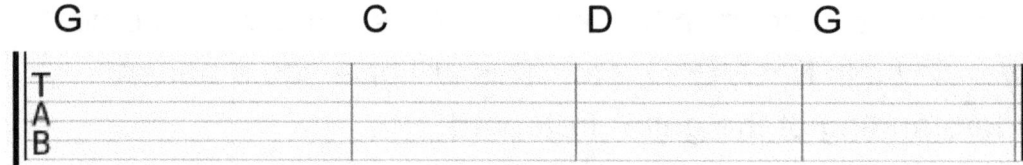

A simple three chord progression in G major that you can solo over in either G major or its relative minor.

Example #2

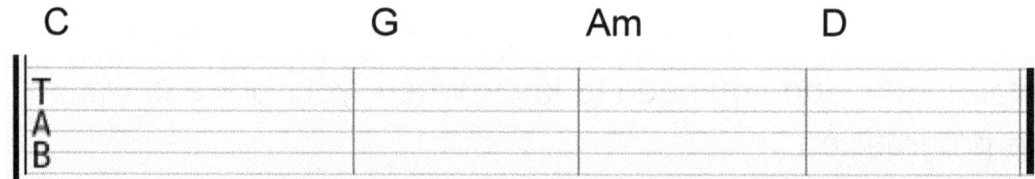

Here is a simple four chord progression that you can solo over at the 8th position in C.

Example #3

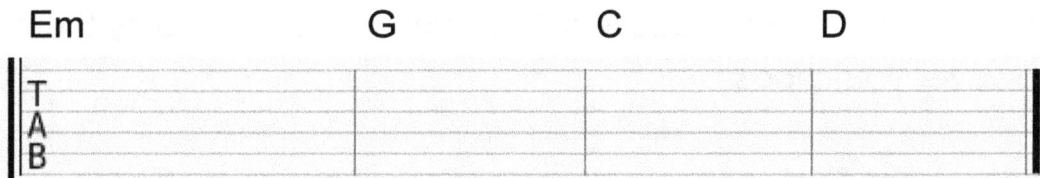

Here is a simple progression that you can play and solo over in both E minor or G major.

Example #4

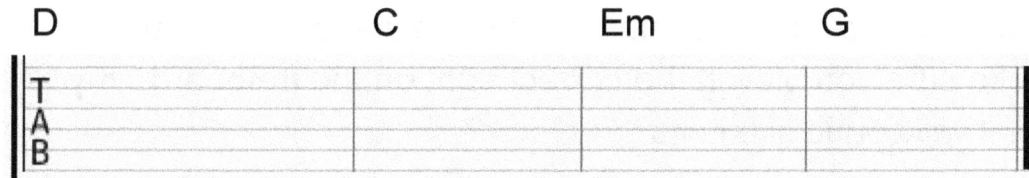

Here is a simple progression in D that you can play and solo over.

Example #5

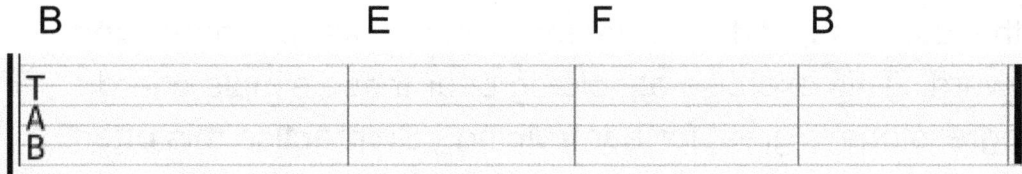

Here is a nice simple three chord progression in B that you can play and solo over.

I have presented you with five simple progressions in different keys that you can practice soloing over. I didn't put any timing sequences in them because it gives you a chance to play them however you choose.

I recommend you go through the chord progressions first to hear how the chords work together. Then either loop it with a looper pedal, record it a few times through with your phone, or with your computer.

Then start soloing over the progression. Listen for how the notes you play in the scales fit over the chord progression. Make sure you play in the correct spot on the fretboard. If you do, it will sound like it fits.

If you are in the wrong location (which you shouldn't be if you have gone through these lessons like you should have) you'll hear how some of the notes don't fit. Listen for this as it is a sign that lets you know you're in the wrong place.

If this happens, find the right location and keep progressing forward. This exercise of soloing over these simple chord progressions is great for ear training. So practice this often.

Chapter 8 Summary

In this chapter we have covered some techniques that will help you with improvising. This is the skill of creating a solo on the spot. Very important to master. All great lead guitar players do this and you can too. But you must put in daily practice.

First we look at guitar licks. Remember, guitar licks are what solos and melody lines are made up of. They're when you put techniques like hammer-ons, pull-offs, bends, slides, vibrato, together to create statements of music.

Just like a writer who uses words to create sentences and paragraphs, you must do the same thing with guitar licks. Use the examples that I have presented as a starting point, then create some of your own.

This is also where learning guitar solos from recordings of your favorite players comes in handy. It teaches you how to create guitar solos. I recommend you don't overlook this.

Once you can put this concept into action in one key, learn to transpose into other keys. Remember, transposing is when you can play in different keys. This is important to learn as well because you never know what key you might need to solo in.

Plus if you write your own songs, you might want to write them in different keys. So knowing how to transpose is going to be a huge benefit in your playing.

It will also give you more knowledge of the guitar fretboard. The keys are all located in different positions. The better you know these the faster you will be able to find where you need to play. Very helpful when it comes to creating a guitar solo.

Arpeggios are another technique that is popular with guitar solos. But in order to really play them well and understand how they work, you need to understand chords. The reason for this is because they are created from the notes in chords.

Chords reside all over the fretboard. And if you learn your notes and how chords work, you'll see them within the scale patterns. Then you can use these notes to create arpeggios whenever you choose to do so.

Use the examples that I have presented as a starting point and see where you can find these in some of the other scale patterns. These are a bit more advanced and will require you to study and practice more to get them down properly.

Another very important skill to develop as a lead guitar player is alternate and tremolo picking. This is how you build speed, accuracy, and stamina in your playing. This is vital for being able to execute certain musical passages.

The technique of alternate picking can also help you in your rhythm playing as well. So I recommend you don't overlook this lesson. If you do, you will find later down the line that your playing will be hindered.

Once you get tremolo picking down you then want to build it up to tremolo picking. This is like putting the pedal to the metal in a car. It allows you to play really fast, and I do mean really fast.

These two techniques are very, very common in guitar solos. And like all the other techniques I've taught you in this book, you will know them when you hear them. And when you do, you'll go "wow, I've got to learn to do that!"

And last but by far not least, chord progressions to solo over. This is where the rubber meets the road. This is where you find out if all I've taught you in this training actually works.

Of course it does, because this is how I learned and how I play so I know that it works. And if you go through it page by page lesson by lesson, you too will find that it works. Just as I have taught it to you.

Knowing how to put chords together to create progressions is very important as a lead guitar player. I know it sounds weird, but it is. Having a solid foundation of rhythm and chords is going to make you a better lead guitar player.

Why?

Because this is what you will solo over. Unless you play an acapella guitar solo, but that is only if you can get to that level. I presented it in this book because it is fun to do, but it takes a lot of practice to be able to do that.

Since this is a beginner book, focus on the basics first. That will come later. Now as I mentioned, work with the chord progressions I have shown in this chapter and learn to solo over them.

Since they are presented in different keys, they will also help you with improvising guitar licks, transposing, rhythm, timing development, and all vital skills needed as a lead guitar player. Who specializes in playing guitar solos and melody lines.

It is one thing to be able to duplicate what is written, but it is something else to create a solo on the spot. Work at mastering both of these skills, and you'll become a force to be reckoned with. I guarantee it!

How To Play Guitar Solos Quiz

Playing lead guitar and being good at improvising and staying in key is something that requires a lot of work. Test yourself to see how well you've done. If you don't know something don't worry, just go back to the chapter and review it.

Q: What is a guitar scale?
A: _____

Q: What does a lead guitar player specialize in?
A: _____

Q: What foundation scales do you need to know?
A: _____

Q: Why is reading tabs beneficial to your guitar playing?
A: _____

Q: What is the benefit of doing finger exercises?
A: _____

Q: What is the note formula for the major pentatonic scale?
A: _____

Q: What does the word pentatonic mean?
A: _____

Q: How many pentatonic scales are there?
A: _____

Q: How many notes are in the pentatonic scale?
A: _____

Q: Why use the pentatonic scale for solos?
A: _____

Q: What is the note formula for the minor pentatonic scale?
A: _____

Q: Where is the A minor pentatonic scale located?
A: _____

Q: Where is the D minor pentatonic scale located?
A: _____

Q: Where is the G major pentatonic scale located?
A: _____

Q: What's the difference between major and minor pentatonic?
A: _____

Q: What is a hammer-on?
A: _____

Q: What is a pull-off?
A: _____

Q: Why use bends and slides in guitar solos?
A: _____

Q; What is vibrato, and what is a trill?
A: _____

Q; where is the first place you can play a solo in a song?
A: _____

Q: Where is the most common place to play a solo in a song?
A: _____

Q: Where else can you play a guitar solo in a song?
A: _____

Q: What's it mean to play a solo by yourself outside of a song?
A: _____

Q: What does it mean to harmonize?
A: _____

Q: What are the 10 most common keys to play in?
A: _____

Q: Why is it important to know where to play?
A: _____

Q: Why is learning guitar solos from recordings beneficial?
A: _____

Q: What is the benefit of developing good solid practice habits?
A: _____

Q: How does looping benefit your learning of songs and solos?
A: _____

Q: What are guitar pedals and why use them?
A: _____

Q: What are some of the most popular guitar pedals to use?
A: _____

Q: What are guitar licks and how do they help your solos?
A: _____

Q: What does the word transposing mean?
A: _____

Q: What are arpeggios, and why use them?
A: _____

Q: What is alternate picking and why learn it?
A: _____

Q: What is tremolo picking and why is it beneficial to develop?
A: _____

Q: What are chord progressions?
A: _____

Q: What is the 12 bar blues progression?
A: _____

Q: What is a turnaround in a 12 bar blues progression?
A: _____

Q: How many chords are commonly found in many songs?
A: _____

Congratulations on taking the test. How did you do? If you did your homework I'm sure you aced it. Great job! If not, don't worry just keep studying. I promise you it will get easier and make more sense as time goes on.

124

How To Play Guitar Solos Conclusion

If you've made it this far I congratulate you on your efforts and say "thank you for your time and purchase of this book". You seem like a student that I'd love to teach in person.

In this book you have learned many things about what it takes to play guitar solos. You've also developed a firm grasp of fundamental concepts and principles that make up music in general.

This book does not teach you everything about playing guitar solos. If it did, it would be the size of a phone book. That is not the objective. The objective is to get you started playing and knowing what to play, where to play, and how to play.

Remember, don't overlook the pentatonic scales. They can teach you a lot and just about every guitar solo has them in it. You just need to learn the 5 scale patterns and focus on where to play them within a certain key, major or minor.

Do this, and you'll be in key every time you play a solo. Then you focus on the guitar licks and techniques needed to bring them to life. Before you know it, you'll be sounding like a rock star! But you must study and practice on a daily basis.

I cannot emphasise this enough, being a great lead guitar player takes more study than just playing rhythm guitar. You must study more, practice more, and develop more dedication and commitment to the instrument.

If you struggle at times, go back through and review the lesson you're having issues with. It will come to you. It took me a while to get it all figured out myself. But I stayed committed to the course and it eventually clicked. It will for you too.

And remember, if you need additional help with any of the lessons I teach in this book, feel free to shoot me an email through my website at Dwayne's Guitar Lessons and I will be happy to help you.

I only wish I had someone like that when I was studying out of books. But of course the internet wasn't developed yet. So be sure to take advantage of the opportunity to reach out if need be. I also teach online lessons through FaceTime & Skype.

Also, follow me on Social Media for my latest lesson updates, and subscribe to my YouTube channel.

Best of luck and most of all, have fun!

Sincerely, Dwayne Jenkins
Tritone Publishing. copyright © 2020

Other Books That Can Help You

In addition to this book, I have authored other books that can help you enjoy playing guitar. If you need help with rhythm, I recommend the book:

Rhythm Guitar Alchemy

A simple step-by-step method book on the science of playing rhythm guitar. It will teach you how to enhance your rhythm skills, which will help you to improve your guitar solo skills.

If you'd like to take your guitar solos to the next level with additional scales, techniques, and lead guitar concepts, I recommend the book:

Lead Guitar Wizardry vol 2:

This book teaches more advanced lead guitar concepts. Such as a comprehensive introduction to the modes, scale note formulas, other minor scales, and music theory.

These two books can help you with your guitar solos in two ways.

1. Your rhythm guitar playing, which is vital to being a great lead guitar player.
2. Enhanced lead guitar education by learning more about scales and advanced techniques.

Having a solid foundation of rhythm is important as it is the foundation of any song. No matter if it is Rock, Country Jazz, Pop, etc. Having a good understanding of chords and rhythm will help your guitar solos.

Learning about modes, additional scales, and scale note formulas will help you to develop a better understanding of how to create guitar solos. As well as enhance your knowledge of the guitar fretboard and music theory.

Both of these books can be purchased through Amazon or through my eBay store. If purchased through my eBay store, you will receive a "personally signed to you" author copy.

If you need more help in these two areas, these two books will do the job and teach you a wealth of information that most guitar players never learn.

130

Video Lesson Library:

Along with teaching private guitar lessons throughout Denver Colorado, providing online lessons, training guides, & blog posts, I also have my video lesson library on Youtube.

In this online library you will find free video lessons on common topics associated with learning to play the guitar. All in simple and easy to understand lesson format.

No matter if a student has just got a guitar and needs to know where to get started, or has already gotten started and feels a bit stuck, my video lessons can help.

Even if you're a student that has been playing for a while and looking to learn more about theory, there is a video lesson here that can guide you in the right direction.

I also have product reviews to help you learn what tools are best to use and help you make a better buying decision. So check out my video lesson library for more information to help your learning.

132

About the Author

Dwayne Jenkins is a professional private guitar teacher and accomplished musician who has been learning, playing and teaching guitar lessons throughout Denver, CO for almost two decades.

He is now bringing his special training skills and methodology that has been honed and hand-crafted throughout the years on how to play guitar to students around the world.

Dwayne has a unique exciting approach that gets students of all ages and skill levels enjoying the fun of playing guitar. His enthusiasm and love for teaching shine through with every lesson that he creates.

His lessons are designed to enhance your ability to progress. No matter your reason for learning guitar, there will always be something in Dwayne's guitar books and products to help you achieve your dreams.

So if you're a student looking to start, or a student looking to further your education, be sure to get involved with Dwayne's guitar lessons.

What Students Are Saying About Dwayne's Guitar Lessons

"Dwayne, thank you so much for everything you have taught me and done for me. You are an amazing guitarist and wonderful teacher" BJ

"Dwayne, it has been a true pleasure to have you at our house each week! Ken & Trevor have learned so much through you and your teachings. Thank you!" Lisa

"Dwayne, thank you for being a great teacher and teaching me many great songs. This is a skill that will last me a lifetime." Danielle

"Dwayne, we want you to know we are honored to have you at the studio. We appreciate all that you do and are grateful that we can leave you in charge" Angie & Wilson M.E.C

"Dwayne, we are so glad you are our Teacher. It's been three years already, can you believe it? Thank you again. You're the best!" Chelsey & Lucas

"Dwayne, we are so glad that you are in our lives. Chelsey & Lucas really enjoy their time with you, and look up to you. Looking forward to another great year!" Love and best wishes, Ken & Sue.

"Dwayne, thank you so much for being not only an awesome guitar teacher, but an awesome friend as well" Kayla

"Dwayne, thank you so much for all the years of doing lessons. You have been very patient with my progress and helped me to build confidence in myself and inspired me to follow my dreams. And in doing so you have become a great friend" Jake

"Dwayne, thank you for teaching Nick guitar so well. He loves it and is getting quite good really fast. I'm amazed!" Jane

"Dwayne, Thank you so much for teaching me every Saturday and not only teaching me guitar but also about life and helping me with setting my goals. You are a great teacher, mentor and the best friend ever" Carson

"There is not another person I would want to be teaching me guitar! His 1 on 1 teaching makes learning guitar very personal & exhilarating. He teaches at your pace and takes pride in what YOU want to learn. The best part...if Dwayne doesn't know a song a student wants to play, he takes time out of the week to learn it. His teaching comes to life in my performance and has progressed over the last 8 years. Words cannot describe how amazing a teacher, rockstar and true friend Dwayne has become to me" Dominic